# THE
# COLORFUL
# CHARACTERS
## OF ST. LOUIS

## JIM MERKEL

REEDY PRESS

Reedy Press
PO Box 5131
St. Louis, MO 63139, USA

Library of Congress Control Number: 2016940394

ISBN: 9781681060491

Cover design by Jill Halpin

Please visit us at jimmerkelthewriter.com
Facebook: Jim Merkel the Writer

Printed in the United States of America

19 20 21 22 23   5 4 3 2

# CONTENTS

## Entertainers

## Sports Guys

## Rebels with a Cause

## Politicos

## Mavericks & Renegades

# INTRODUCTION

Tom Goabout must have had a one-track mind. Why else would he spend the two decades after 1885 doing little else but stealing chickens and dogs? He was good at it, to be sure, otherwise the *St. Louis Post-Dispatch* wouldn't have devoted seventy or so articles to Tom Goabout and his unusual profession. But the only explanation for why he didn't diversify much has to be that he was obsessed. And why does Bill Haas, everybody's favorite perennial candidate, put his name up for election to major office year after year? Again, obsession must play a part. Why has a man spent years on a bridge over Interstate 44 in Webster Groves, waving at motorists below? Once more, obsession. But that's not a bad thing.

That word, used to describe three of the colorful characters profiled in this book, needn't be negative. An online dictionary and thesaurus uses these positive alternative words for obsession: "craving, desire, drive, enthusiasm, fascination, hankering, hunger, infatuation, itch, longing, lust, passion, pining, thirst, urge, yearning, yen, idiosyncrasy, quirk, bent, disposition, inclination, leaning, penchant, predilection, predisposition, proclivity, propensity, tendency." The words tell of people born with a certain determination, a focus that others don't have. When we encounter them, we take a second look and say, "What was that?" The answer, of course, is another colorful character.

The online dictionary and thesaurus consulted above describes "colorful character" as "a very unusual person." Colorful characters may be obsessive, but they don't have to be. A certain style might be enough, a forcefulness. Colorful characters have a sort of tick about them that makes it impossible to ignore them. Their job description would be "keeping things from getting boring." The all-time champion American colorful character has to be Teddy Roosevelt.

You know that loose banister post George Bailey pulls out every time he walks up the stairs of his house in *It's a Wonderful Life*? If it were a human being, it would be a colorful character. In the same movie, Clarence would be a colorful character, but George Bailey wouldn't be. At the core, he was a hard-working guy who gave up his dreams for his hometown. It's praiseworthy and worth putting in a book, but not this one. So it was with the profiles in the book. People may be eminently successful or have a compelling story, but they may not be worth telling here, so they were dropped.

Many of the stories herein are funny enough to make readers cackle and slap their legs. But not all of them. Civil rights advocate Percy Green isn't much at cracking a smile, but he earned a place in the volume because of his own style. His climb up 125 feet of the Gateway Arch and his involvement in the unmasking of the Veiled Prophet made history. Others would have different definitions of colorful character and might include different people. The one in this book is as good as any.

We were able to include just about everybody we wanted in this book but not all. Once I was stuck in traffic at a major intersection in South St. Louis when I saw the most amazing sight. It was Gandalf, or a reasonable approximation of the guy in *The Lord of the Rings* movies, complete with walking stick and long, flowing white gown, the whole package, standing imposingly at the street corner. I had to interview him, right there. When the light turned green, I drove through the intersection, parked, and walked back. It couldn't have been more than two or three minutes. I don't know where he went, but he was gone. Vanished. A couple of weeks later, the same thing happened. I was at a major street corner when I again spotted Gandalf. I pulled over as soon as I could, then ran back. He was gone! Once again, I had no idea where he went. If I had only been able to interview him, I surely could have written a fantastic essay. If you see him, hold him down with his walking stick and call me. There may be a second edition, and I want him in it.

# MEDIA MAVENS

# William Reedy:
# A *Mirror* to St. Louis

Villiam Marion Reedy had a different kind of training to edit the nation's leading magazine of opinion, politics, and literature. The son of an Irish police sergeant, born during the Civil War in St. Louis's Irish Kerry Patch neighborhood, he honed his skill as a writer from 1880 to 1893 reporting for the *Missouri Republican* and the *St. Louis Globe-Democrat*. It was a time when reporters competed for the juiciest headline about their rough-and-tumble town. A big man, Reedy learned well. As editor of the St. Louis–based *Reedy's Mirror* from 1893 until 1920, he passed judgment on submissions from the best writers of his time.

Reedy was as responsible as anyone for making Nathaniel Hawthorne and Emily Dickinson required reading among today's high school students. The works of Carl Sandburg, William Butler Yeats, Stephen Crane, and others now considered writers of classics appeared in the *Mirror*. He discovered the poet Edgar Lee Masters and first published Masters's masterpiece, *Spoon River Anthology*. Reedy was a regular guest at President Theodore Roosevelt's White House. With more than thirty-two thousand copies read throughout the United States, the circulation of *Reedy's Mirror* far outstripped the

*Nation* (twelve thousand) and the *Atlantic* (five thousand). Reedy's influence lives on in still-read works that appeared in the weekly. It's also seen in the publishing house Reedy Press, whose founders chose the name because they sought to publish the kind of works of literary consequence that William Reedy printed in his *Mirror*.

Everywhere, people learned from Reedy about the latest political shenanigans in St. Louis, Missouri, and the nation. "There are men who have talked more of modern democracy," Reedy said of Joe Folk, who cleaned political house with a Paul Bunyan–sized broom first as St. Louis circuit attorney and then as governor. But, Reedy continued, "There is none who has done more." In an 1899 essay titled "What's the Matter with St. Louis? An Attempt at a Diagnosis of a Generally Observed Ailment in the Fourth City of the Union," Reedy reviewed some of the city's symptoms before saying: "This brings us to the chief deficiency of St. Louis, which accounts for the poor, almost ridiculous, position of the city in the minds of the country at large: There is no civic pride in St. Louisans." He died at the age of fifty-seven in San Francisco, where he had gone to attend the 1920 Democratic convention. In its obituary, the *Post-Dispatch* noted a self-deprecating remark Reedy had made in one of his many speeches, about speaking at "this large and respectable gathering—I am large, and you are respectable."

# Bill Mauldin: Point Man for the Soldier

For anyone else, winning a Pulitzer Prize in editorial cartooning would seem to be a career-high event. But when it happened to *Post-Dispatch* cartoonist Bill Mauldin in 1959, it was a matter of the second time around. Mauldin was already the hero of all GIs when he won the Pulitzer Prize in 1945 for the beloved *Willie and Joe* cartoons about two soldiers fighting to survive in World War II. People had reacted that way to Mauldin's artwork as long as he was drawing, and that was a long time. Even before he went to school in Mountain Park, New Mexico, in the 1920s, he carried around the pencil and paper he needed to make his drawings. His doodling in class galled his teachers, but classmates loved the way he drew perfect pictures of Donald Duck and Mickey Mouse. He was on his way to a career in cartooning when the war changed everything.

Mauldin joined the Arizona National Guard in 1940 and quickly found himself taken off latrine duty on Friday afternoons to draw a weekly cartoon for the *45th Division News*. From his first cartoon, showing soldiers peeling potatoes, he made fun of military life. Early on, he drew characters who would become Willie and Joe, two bedraggled, everyman soldiers, marching, surrounded by destroyed buildings, always sinking in mud, always looking tired. One showed the two sitting in a field full of mud. "Joe, yesiddy ya saved my life an' I swore I'd pay ya back," Willie says. "Here's my last pair o' dry socks." As soldiers moved forward, Mauldin went with them as just another guy on the front. His cartoons showed up in another military paper, *Stars and Stripes*. Soldiers loved it, but General George S. Patton Jr. hated the depiction of two slovenly soldiers who never seemed to shave. Fortunately, General Dwight Eisenhower backed Mauldin, who was still drawing when Germany surrendered.

The war over, Mauldin retired Willie and Joe and concentrated on issues of the day as a political cartoonist for United Features Syndicate. He quit in 1948 and generally drifted for the decade after that. He wrote books, including one about an up-close tour of the Korean War front, acted in a film version of Stephen Crane's *The Red Badge of Courage,* and lost a bid for a seat in Congress. But he didn't focus on one thing until 1958, when he heard about an opening for a cartoonist at the *St. Louis Post-Dispatch.*

Mauldin always thought the liberal *Post-Dispatch* was one of the greatest papers in the country, and he jumped at the chance. At night in bed in his home in Frontenac, Mauldin surrounded himself with pencils, newspapers, magazines, and a stenographer's notepad and started drawing several cartoons about various news items. In the shower the next morning, coffee in his hand, he chose one possibility. At work that morning, he pitched the idea to editorial page editor Robert Lasch. With Lasch's okay, he spent the next four hours crafting his picture of the day. The exhausting process paid off. He skewered local politicians, while providing sharp critiques on such national issues as civil rights and nuclear weapons.

One cartoon won Mauldin the 1959 Pulitzer Prize. Mauldin's subject was the refusal of Soviet authorities to allow author Boris Pasternak to accept the Nobel Prize in literature. His cartoon showed two prisoners in a snowy Siberian gulag talking to each other. "I won the Nobel Prize for Literature. What was your crime?" one said. His popularity was not enough to keep him in St. Louis. In 1962, Mauldin left the *Post-Dispatch* for the *Chicago Sun-Times* because the owners of the *Post-Dispatch* wouldn't match the *Sun-Times*'s pay.

With the move to Chicago, Mauldin built a national reputation for his political cartooning. He penned perhaps his most compelling political cartoon on the day President Kennedy was assassinated by depicting President Abraham Lincoln weeping into his hands at the Lincoln Memorial. He traveled to Vietnam and was a regular visitor to President Lyndon Johnson's ranch until he turned against the Vietnam War. But gradually, he drifted again. He reduced his output from four to three cartoons a week in 1983. In 1990, the *Sun-Times* eliminated his cartoon for financial reasons. He visited troops fighting in the 1990–1991 Persian Gulf War. When news came that he was dying, veterans everywhere sent sacks full of letters to his nursing home in Newport Beach, California. His list of accomplishments, including those in St. Louis, was long by the time he died in 2003 at the age of eighty-one. But what everyone remembered him for was the way he made the life of the ordinary soldier real in his cartoons of two ordinary guys named Willie and Joe.

# Robert Hyland: The Boss Who Never Slept

In most places, the early morning shift is the place to be to avoid the boss's eye. Not so at KMOX when Bob Hyland worked as the station's general manager and senior vice president of CBS Radio. "If you did something wrong, the phone was going to ring," said Frank Absher, who was a KMOX utility announcer from 1979 to 1983. By Absher's account, Hyland relied on paid blind listeners to let him know when an announcer mispronounced a local surname in the dead of night. It helped that Hyland slept only four hours a night—from 9 p.m. to 1 a.m.—got into work at 2 a.m., and always tuned his radio to 1120 AM. Hyland's tireless, almost manic, management style was bad news for workers who didn't measure up to his standards, but it also made the station's slogan, "The Voice of St. Louis," not just nice advertising but a nationally recognized fact.

Hyland's training as a 24/7 boss began in a fourteen-room Central West End apartment. He was born in 1920, the son of Dr. Robert Hyland Sr., team physician for the St. Louis Cardinals and the old St. Louis Browns. The junior Hyland worshipped his father, who in turn kept him under his thumb. After Hyland graduated from St. Louis University, his mother nixed a Cardinals minor league contract offer. She wanted him to focus on business. Meanwhile, his father opposed an opportunity for him to go into the movies. Instead, he got into radio announcing and sales at stations in Quincy, Illinois, and Chicago before coming to KMOX as a salesman. He worked up to KMOX general station manager in 1955 and a CBS vice president in 1959.

Hyland molded KMOX into a station all would respect. He introduced a new call-in format, called "At Your Service." With big names like nationally known sports broadcaster Jack Buck and superstar broadcaster Jack Carney, KMOX became the unquestioned leader in St. Louis radio. Hyland cemented the station's reputation as a sports powerhouse, locking in coverage of the baseball and football Cardinals, Blues hockey, and the old St. Louis Hawks basketball team.

"Do what you gotta do. Don't bother with the details," was Hyland's modus operandi, Absher said. That dedication showed itself on March 30, 1981, when news came that President Ronald Reagan had been shot. "Throw out all the commercials. Do whatever it takes. Don't worry about the cost. I want it to be the best," Hyland said. Dumping commercials cost KMOX thousands, but the coverage of the attempted assassination was as good as anybody's.

Absher, who now is executive director of the St. Louis Media History Foundation, saw that dedication again in the last weekend of the 1982 baseball season, after the Redbirds clinched a spot in the playoffs. Three games played simultaneously would determine other playoff berths. Hyland ordered live phone feeds for all three games. With an earphone in one ear giving a game's play-by-play and a phone to Hyland in the other, Absher switched from one game to another. "He loved doing things like that. We had a ball," Absher said.

Hyland's overpowering presence earned him enemies who claimed he was a tyrant. After he died in 1992, *Riverfront Times* columnist Ed Bishop wrote that as a reporter he had to call Hyland at 5 a.m. to reach him. "I had the feeling he was afraid not to be there, as if he would somehow lose control. Apparently, control over people's lives was a big part of Hyland's life," Bishop wrote. For his part, Carney said he'd worry if his boss didn't attract his share of opprobrium. "To this day, I would walk through the jaws of hell for him," Carney confided. If that happened, Hyland likely would send a crew to cover Carney's trip.

# Dana Brown: Tiger Hunter, Coffee Seller

For anybody else, Dana Brown's kitschy ads for Safari Coffee might get an ad agency pitchman fired. Or a whole ad agency. But Dana Brown was the pitchman *and* the ad agency, and his ads sold enough cans of coffee to leave $45 million to a charitable trust when he died in 1994. The TV ads for Safari Coffee showed pictures and snippets of movies about his exploits on safaris. But the bachelor hunter didn't make the two- or three-month jaunts to exotic lands just because he liked it. He saw it as the way to sell coffee, and he knew a lot about selling.

He was as good as they came at making a deal. But it didn't seem like he'd be selling at the beginning of his life. He worked as a lumberjack in West Virginia as a teenager, lived the life of a hobo, and drove spikes on the railroad. In Toledo, Ohio, he found his calling as a door-to-door salesman selling Fuller Brushes. "Good" wasn't a strong enough word to describe his skills in persuading housewives to surrender money to him in exchange for brushes.

Brown then turned to using his sales acumen in hawking coffee for private label brands, which

provided coffee sold by others under their own brands, such as a supermarket chain. In 1955, he became president of General Grocers Co.'s Manhattan Coffee Co. in St. Louis. He bought the company in 1958 for in excess of $2,500,000. He became rich when he sold the firm to Nestlé Co., a Swiss conglomerate. He managed the firm for seven more years, using footage of his safaris in commercials. But when Nestlé complained that he was spending too much time on safaris, Brown decided it was grounds for a split. "I tried to tell them that it was my safari pictures and stories that were selling the coffee, but they wouldn't listen," Brown told reporter John M. McGuire in 1979. "It was the romance and adventure that did it." He formed his own private label company, Dana Brown Private Brands, Inc., and was quickly perking along. That firm roasted and packed coffee in Houston. Until he sold the company in 1991, he was a major force in St. Louis's coffee business.

Romance and adventure weren't the words to describe Brown's frequent ventures into conservative politics, especially when it came to Africa. He ran full-page ads in St. Louis's two newspapers condemning American policy toward Rhodesia, now Zimbabwe. His wall contained an autographed photo of former Rhodesian prime minister Ian Smith and a map of Africa covered with thumbtacks showing where he thought there was communist influence. Locally, he opposed efforts to tear down buildings to make way for the first Busch Memorial Stadium downtown.

It was enough to make this hunter of coffee sales worry, but not enough to remove his smile while he was out hunting. From his first safari in 1953 to his last in 1989, he made twenty-five jaunts to Africa and nine to Nepal. Brown, who died in 1994, claimed that in a trip to Africa in 1975, he hung upside down for a half-hour from a snare trap. Back at his St. Louis office, zebra and tiger skins covered the floor and elephant tusks and animal heads the wall. In a TV studio made to look like a safari camp, he reminded those at home of his coffee's great taste. The IRS fought him over it, but he was able to write off his safaris as a business expense. He was after big game, and there was no bigger game than a fat bottom line.

# Don "Johnny Rabbitt" Pietromonaco: Bruno and Friend

When disc jockey Don Pietromonaco came in for work at KXOK evenings in the 1960s, he brought in two cups of coffee. One was for himself and one for a scruffy, frantic, juvenile delinquent imaginary friend named Bruno J. Grunion. The swarms of teenagers who tuned in as Pietromonaco spoke for himself and the high-pitched gravel-voiced Bruno from 1964 to 1969 still remember them as a legendary AM radio team. Pietromonaco was so good that many listeners thought Bruno actually existed, rather than being a sidekick in the style of Edgar Bergen's Charlie McCarthy. From the KXOK studio, he painted a vivid picture that St. Louis baby boomers still remember. "He knew the power of the theater of the mind," said St. Louis native Jonnie King, a longtime actor, broadcaster, webmaster, and close friend of Pietromonaco.

Pietromonaco was the second KXOK deejay to have the name Johnny Rabbitt. Ron Elz went by it from 1962 to 1964, when he left KXOK, and used it again after Pietromonaco departed. Since then, Elz has gone by Johnny Rabbitt as a popular local writer, broadcaster, and historian. Elz started in radio in 1954 at the age of 15, has been on numerous local radio stations, and now deejays the oldies show Route 66 on KMOX. He's been inducted into the DJ section of the Rock & Roll Hall of Fame in Cleveland. But today, Pietromonaco retains a solid following in St. Louis. His success was no accident. Pietromonaco wasn't just a radio guy but an accomplished movie actor who started as a child. After a talent scout discovered him—really—performing in a play on Hollywood Boulevard, Pietromonaco got a role in Bertolt Brecht's *Galileo* starring Charles Laughton. That led to child roles in such movies as *An Affair to Remember* and *The Boy with Green Hair*. He went into the army and joined the same unit Elvis Presley was in. Setting his eyes on a career behind the mike, he worked his way up to KRIZ in Phoenix, Arizona. Then KXOK hired him, gave him the night shift, and told him to reel in the kids. The dial was still on KXOK when parents flipped on the radio in the morning. Pietromonaco quickly dominated the city's nighttime ratings and wouldn't relinquish them for years. In the late sixties, KXOK became the number one independent station in the United States.

"He was extraordinarily talented in two-voice repartee back and forth," said Bud Connell, who was KXOK operations manager for much of the time Pietromonaco worked there. "It was like a situation comedy of radio. Characters were in and out"—characters as bizarre as a man-eating plant shared time with Bruno and the Rabbitt. They called Bruno the "Purple Pizza Eater," after a popular song about an alien, the "Purple People Eater." At other times, he taped Bruno's side in advance and then talked back to the tape when the mike was live. "He could say stuff that Rabbitt couldn't say," said Tim Neeley, a longtime friend of Pietromonaco and administrator of the Facebook closed group KXOK 630 AM Radio St. Louis Flashback.

Pietromonaco often staged "Rabbitt Hops" on Sunday nights at the Club Imperial at Goodfellow Boulevard and West Florissant Avenue. In the basement was "Bruno's Bat Cave," in homage to the popularity of the *Batman* TV series. The Bat Cave was a stop for such groups as Sam the Sham and the Pharoahs and Gayle

McCormick and the Klassmen. He kept another place called Cloud Nyne. When big names like Sammy Davis Jr. came into town, Pietromonaco was there to greet them. Public appearances filled Pietromonaco's calendar, and he often made friends through them. "He would refer to himself a lot of times as the Pied Piper of St. Louis because teenagers followed him everywhere," Neeley said. Neeley was about twelve when Pietromonaco met him at an appearance. He soon was with him at the studio and backstage with him at concerts.

People loved Pietromonaco but not the management that came in late in his tenure at KXOK. Pietromonaco hated it so much that he quit in 1969 and went back to KRIZ. From there, he returned to Los Angeles, where he did commercials and taught voiceover techniques for radio and television ads. He had a chance to start broadcasting again in St. Louis, but he wanted to do it from Los Angeles. The station wouldn't buy it, and Pietromonaco's voice stayed out of St. Louis. He kept up with friends and family members in St. Louis, who were saddened to learn in 1997 that he had died at the age of sixty-one of complications from emphysema. To his fans, it wasn't just Don Pietromonaco who had passed on but Bruno J. Grunion and a world of fun they knew when they were growing up in St. Louis.

# Amadee Wohlschlaeger: Fifty-Nine Years a Weatherbird

Amadee Wohlschlaeger was a big man who loved to draw his artwork with a cigar in his mouth and a scotch nearby. The busy, overwhelming tone of the artwork he produced for the *Post-Dispatch* from 1932 to 1981 matched his own pace and overwhelming presence. "The term 'larger than life' really applies to him," said Dan Martin, who started drawing the Weatherbird in 1986. "He really was just a force of nature." Wohlschlaeger loved people, and he loved his artwork. "All I ever wanted to do was draw, from kindergarten on. I was born to be an artist," he said.

Wohlschlaeger attended St. Boniface Catholic School in the city's Carondelet neighborhood, skipped high school, and spent two semesters studying art and design at Washington University. After that, his father, a *Post-Dispatch* printer and linotype machine operator, got him a job in the paper's art department. Opportunity came when Weatherbird artist Carlisle Martin died in 1932. Wohlschlaeger worked until 2 a.m. crafting a dozen drawings of the Weatherbird, which began life as a front-page commentator on the news in 1901. The features editor took a look at the samples and hired him at the age of twenty-one.

With mighty hands, Wohlschlaeger sometimes dashed off two, three, or more of the *Post-Dispatch* Weatherbird front-page drawings a day. He regularly made detailed drawings of the previous day's Cardinals games, did spot illustrations for the feature and food sections, and penned numerous portraits of ballplayers and artwork for sports columnists. He spent a month as the paper's editorial cartoonist in 1939 and ten years in the 1940s and 1950s doing a comic strip without words. In his spare time, he kept himself busy doing artwork for freelance clients ranging from the *Sporting News* to McDonald's and Hardee's.

The demands of Wohlschlaeger's job would wear out anyone who didn't share his enthusiasm and love of the life of an artist. In the days when the paper was printed in the afternoon, he went to the stadium press box when there was a night game and made drawings until the game was over about 10 p.m. He drove to his home in Sunset Hills and finished the drawings around 1 or 2 a.m. When he was done, he slept a while and then got up in time to drive the artwork to his office by an 8 a.m. deadline. He next turned his attention to other tasks, including producing Weatherbirds seven days a week. When there were five editions in a day, he often produced new drawings for different editions to match changing front-page content. One day, he actually did five different drawings. The tone of the drawings was often frantic, as in his aerial view of the old Busch Stadium for the 1957 All-Star Game. Readers saw a smiling Cardinal flying over the stadium, a passenger train, airplanes, the Anheuser-Busch brewery, Forest Park, and huge figures of Cardinals owner August A. (Gussie) Busch and Cardinals broadcasters Harry Caray and Joe Garagiola.

As busy as he was, Wohlschlaeger took time out to schmooze with the likes of Busch on his yearly trips to illustrate the Cardinals' spring training in St. Petersburg, Florida. Amadee often fished off the pier used by Gussie Busch. "Hey, pal," Busch often would cry. That meant it was time for some vodka and a fast boat ride. Back at his desk in St. Louis, Amadee wasn't the best speller, and he showed it when he drew a gaggle of turkeys squawking "gooble gooble." This was an opening for sports columnist Bob Broeg to chirp, "Gee, we always thought they gobble goobled." Amadee returned the wiseacre remark with this aside: "Not the turkeys I've known." Another buddy, Cardinals broadcaster Jack Buck, scribbled a poem about Amadee that began, "How many here tonight have been assaulted by an Amadee cigar?" And singer

Tony Bennett once drew Amadee's likeness while hanging out with him in the Cardinals' press box. In return, Wohlschlaeger scrawled a picture of Bennett. The singer eyed it and gave it to broadcaster Mike Shannon. "He didn't like the way I drew his honker," Wohlschlaeger said.

Wohlschlaeger retired in 1981 but kept drawing until 2005. He traveled to all the nation's baseball parks to do illustrations for the *Sporting News* book *Take Me Out to the Ball Park*. Kellogg's put the drawings on the back of its Raisin Bran cereal boxes. After he died at 102 in 2014, two cigars were stuffed into his suit's front pocket when he was laid out at a funeral home. In death, he was as big as ever.

# Jack Carney: The Broadcasting King of St. Louis

So how popular was Jack Carney? What other radio guy could tell his listeners he was planning the I'm Proud to Be an American–I'm Proud to Be a St. Louisan–and No One Ever Asked Me to Be in a Parade Before Parade, and make it wind a mile through Forest Park? Who else could tell jokes on the top of a horse while a sorry company of clowns, marching bands, double-decker buses, sportscasters Jack Buck and Mike Shannon, and the kazoo-playing Mattese Canoeing, Sailing, Skinny Dipping, and Symphonic Band Society followed? "It was the best/worst parade I've ever been to," University City state senator Harriett Woods said after the April 1981 event mercifully ended. Thousands laughed in person, but hundreds of thousands at home chortled when they heard Jack Carney talk about it on KMOX. They tuned to the station for Jack Buck, Bob Costas, and others, but Jack Carney was the guy they went to for pure fun. From 1971 to 1984, he stayed on

top of the ratings when he was on the air and drew about $4 million worth of advertising a year to KMOX. He was king at a station that considered itself broadcasting royalty.

Born in Los Angeles in 1932, Jack Carney deejayed in small towns in Texas and New Mexico before advancing to stations in Phoenix, Galveston, Milwaukee, Atlanta, Boston, and finally WIL in 1958. People credited him with making Bobby Darin's "Mack the Knife" a hit. At WIL, he asked everybody to write "Pookie Snackenberg" on the lower right-hand corner of blackboards. Quickly, the name appeared on blackboards throughout St. Louis. That led to Pookie Snackenberg buttons and T-shirts and Pookie Snackenberg Night at the Casa Loma Ballroom. Versions of a Carney car caper vary. One rush hour, he announced that either a $100 bill or the winning clue for a ten thousand dollar prize was taped to a car radiator cap. Traffic halted as motorists stopped their cars and popped open their hoods to see if they were the winners.

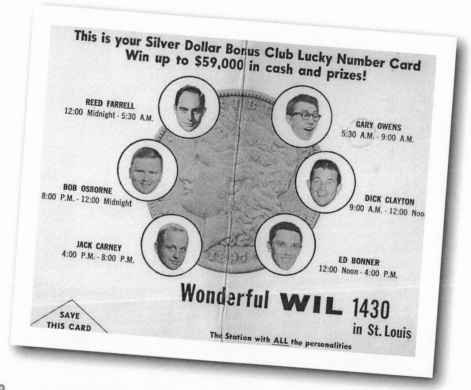

THE COLORFUL CHARACTERS OF ST. LOUIS

Execs at WABC in New York heard how Carney had made WIL number one in St. Louis and hired him away. From there, he went to KSFO in San Francisco. He was popular in San Francisco, but not number one. So he went to KMOX in 1971. "Even though dad did great, I don't think he wanted to be number two in the market," said Jack Carney's son John Carney, a veteran St. Louis broadcaster who works for KTRS Radio.

In St. Louis, national celebrities quickly learned that if they wanted to sell tickets for their event in St. Louis, they had to spend time on Carney's show. He became close to a long list of stars that included Eddie Fisher, Flip Wilson, Tiny Tim, and Robert Goulet. Many of those stars stayed at Carney's house when they came to town. In one show in 1977, Carney fought a no-holds-barred, get-the-most-laughs contest with sausage king Jimmy Dean. They might have traded guffaws for days had station general manager Robert Hyland not decided the banter was too racy for straitlaced listeners in Kirkwood, John Carney recalled. Hyland, who had a reputation as a tyrant, marched into the studio and ordered Dean to leave.

Like many teenagers, John Carney didn't spend much time listening to his father on the air, but he did decide early on that he wanted to go into radio. The elder Carney tried to talk his son out of going into radio because it was dying. John reacted by enrolling in radio school. He started at KSLV in Colorado and then went on to KFRU in Columbia. John Carney was working at KFRU in 1984 when he heard his father had died of a heart attack. The news stunned St. Louisans. Jack Carney could have gone to bigger places, his son said, but he wanted to stay in St. Louis, where he was number one. Besides, he liked it here. "I'm not a Pollyanna who overlooks the faults in St. Louis, but to me the manner of living here is the closest to perfect that I've ever encountered," he once said. He was gold, and St. Louisans considered him a treasure.

# William Barnaby Faherty, SJ: A Wordsmith to the End

The Reverend William Barnaby Faherty wrote books, lots of them, mostly about St. Louis history. To say that the Jesuit priest and St. Louis University history professor cranked out more than fifty books implies his books weren't up to snuff. In fact, they were deep reads, with history that made it clear Faherty knew his subject. One of the biggest things he learned was what Faherty thought about his hometown. "He was very proud of St. Louis, he was very proud of the history of St. Louis," said John Waide, the former archivist at Pius XII Memorial Library at St. Louis University. Whether he was writing a novel that would be made into a movie or a story of St. Louis, he was a star among Gateway City historians.

Faherty's path to becoming one of the greatest keepers of knowledge about St. Louis history started in 1914, when he was born in the family abode on Arsenal Street. His father was from Irish stock that immigrated to southern Illinois in 1851, and his mother descended from German Hungarians. His middle name was "Barby," after his mother's maiden name, but when every girl around started playing with Barbie dolls, he used the word "Barnaby." Early on, he wrote short stories. As a seventh grader at Epiphany Parish School, he penned an essay on St. Louis history that won a contest sponsored by the old *St. Louis Star-Times* newspaper.

Setting his sights on a life in the priesthood, Faherty attended the Jesuit St. Stanislaus Seminary in Florissant in 1931, was ordained in 1944, and received his doctorate from St. Louis University in 1949. In his long career as a Jesuit, he held such posts as history professor at St. Louis University, archivist for the Missouri Jesuit Province, and director of the Jesuits' St. Stanislaus Museum in Florissant. The constant throughout his career was writing.

Faherty's big break nationally was his 1963 novel *A Wall for San Sebastian*, set in Mexico at the start of the nineteenth century. It was adopted into a popular 1968 movie, *Guns for San Sebastian*, starring Anthony Quinn. He wrote about the Jesuits, the Germans, and the Irish in St. Louis, as well as Missouri Botanical Garden founder Henry Shaw. He penned books about women's rights from a Catholic perspective and the launch facilities of the Apollo moon program. He helped write the first Jesuit encyclopedia, covered the city's history in *St. Louis Portrait*, and wrote a history of the first 150 years of St. Louis University.

This kept Faherty busy, but not so busy that he didn't have time for other things. Late in his life, he swam regularly and played tennis. He was as big a Cardinal fan as anybody and once wrote *The Book of Cardinalimericks* with sports cartoonist Amadee Wohlschlaeger. The book dealt with major players from Cardinals world championship teams from 1926 to 1982. So enthralled was he with his Redbirds that he used the chest and waist measurements of an unidentified member of the Cardinals 1934 Gashouse Gang for his security code to get into the Jesuit residence on Lindell Boulevard.

When wives of members of the River des Peres Yacht Club worried that their husbands imbibed too much at club meetings, they dispatched Faherty to be chaplain. Members didn't go boating, but they did enter a wrecked boat on a flatbed truck as a float in a St. Patrick's Day parade. It was, of course, one of the favorite days for this true blue son of Ireland. He loved to wear a shamrock and a green sweater.

Faherty cut back his schedule after he broke his hip several years before he died. While he was confined to a wheelchair, Waide stepped in to drive him on his various errands. Among the stops was St. Louis Catholic radio station WRYT, where Faherty recorded his program *Catholic St. Louis*. When he could no longer go to the station, he recorded the program in his room at St. Louis University. He died at the age of ninety-six on August 22, 2011, just days after taping a program.

"He was still writing things until almost the day he passed away," Waide said. Just before he died, he started another book.

# Steve Mizerany: The King of Schmaltz

In the dawn of the television era, nobody knew about prerecorded commercials. They were live. So when Joe Mizerany decided to buy some TV time for his South Side appliance store, his brother Steve got the job of plugging refrigerators, washers, and dryers for the family store. From that inauspicious beginning came the long reign of Steve Mizerany as the king of schmaltzy commercials that St. Louis TV viewers loved to hate. Schweig Engel and Uncle Leonard had their fans, but don't be confused—nobody on TV was cornier than Steve Mizerany.

Mizerany got his introduction to sales growing up in an apartment above his family's grocery store at Tenth Street and Park Avenue. He was the son of Lebanese immigrants and the youngest of five kids. "I always was a silly guy. I was sort of a nitwit," he said a year before he died in 2011 at the age of eighty-seven. That would be a key throughout his career. So would a boy who lived in the neighborhood by the name of Joe Farhatt. Farhatt worked at the store and became a lifelong friend. When Mizerany went to work after World War II, Joe Farhatt also worked there. He was the one who suggested that Steve Mizerany do commercials. And in the mid-1950s, a foul-up during one of those commercials set a pattern that would go on for decades.

As the cameras rolled, he poured wood alcohol on top of a washer and set it on fire. He wanted to show that the washer wouldn't burn. But a bit of the alcohol dripped down and caught some of the rubber in the washer on fire. Before you could say "Fire Sale!" a backdrop curtain was ablaze. The fire department came out to douse the conflagration. Bad news? No. "It got lots of play," Mizerany said. It moved refrigerators and washers out the door. "Our commercials were so bad that the people liked 'em and bought," he said.

Mizerany kept making the corny ads as the family opened new stores around the St. Louis area. In the early 1970s, Steve Mizerany and Farhatt broke away and formed Mizerany New Deal. In time, it had seven stores, including one next to the Bevo Mill. The Bevo Mill may be a South Side landmark, but not if you listened to Steve Mizerany. "The Bevo Mill is next to us," he'd say in his high-pitched nasal voice. To emphasize that his prices were the lowest, he'd proclaim, "Don't be confused. We don't bait and switch." Dressed on camera in obnoxious plaids and stripes, he'd roller skate past his appliances as he gave his pitches.

A strong Catholic, Mizerany liked to say how God had helped him. He backed numerous charities and once raised more than $39,000 for the family of St. Louis detective Melvin Wilmoth after the officer died in a narcotics raid in 1972. In just two and a half weeks, he once gathered more than twenty-three thousand signatures from registered voters on a petition opposing repeal of blue laws that kept retail stores closed on Sunday. He left the New Deal in Farhatt's hands in 1989, but he later added his voice to spots for Warehouse of Waterbeds, which two of his nieces operated. "If you ain't sleeping on water, you otter," he said. Up to the end, he was known for one slogan. He was weak when an interviewer visited him in 2010 at the Bethesda Meadow nursing home in Ellisville, a year before he died. But when asked, he said with characteristic gusto, "Don't be confused."

# Miriam Blue: Sound Advice from a Cleaning Lady

I t sounds like a tale from an old feel-good movie. A cleaning lady walks into a radio station's studio during a commercial to empty ashtrays. She starts talking to the announcer, not knowing the mike is live. People listening to the banter love her, and she winds up doing a regular advice show with the announcer. Fame comes when outlets like the *Wall Street Journal* and the *Real People* television show feature her. The station adds to her paycheck, but she keeps her main job, sweeping and vacuuming the studios. "I couldn't be happy as the idle rich," she quips.

It wasn't a movie where this happened, but at KMOX radio in the fall of 1975, when station personality Jack Carney put Miriam Blue on the air. From then until the beginning of the 1980s, her simple advice kept listeners close to their radios. She'd come a long way from her beginnings in Corinth, Mississippi. She lived with her grandmother until she died. When she was a teenager, Blue came to St. Louis to live with relatives. At forty-seven, her husband walked out on her and her two children. To keep a roof over their heads and food on their table, she cleaned offices.

"My grandmother told me you had to make your own place in the world," she said. "God promised me daily rations. He never said he was going to give me a rose garden. Even a rose garden had thorns." She found comfort in the biblical story of how Elijah helped a poor widow. To show her faith, she started using the phrase "All is well." Likely, she used those words when she went to work at KMOX's offices at 1 Memorial Drive in 1969.

There are variations in the story of how Miriam Blue's voice first went out over the station's fifty thousand watts during Carney's 9 a.m.-to-1 p.m. program. The constant seems to be that

Carney knew he was live and she didn't. No matter. Soon, at the same time on Tuesdays and Thursdays, she would put down her broom, sit at the mike, and answer letters from the lovelorn. "Is it OK to burn my bra?" queried a woman, unsure about this practice in the women's movement. "Sure," replied the mistress of the mop and the difficult question. "But be sure to take it off first." Always, she added, "A-l-l-l is well." When she once neglected the retort, phone calls jammed the switchboard.

Frank Absher got to know Blue when he was a utility announcer at KMOX from 1979 to 1983. "With Miriam, what you saw was what you got. It came across on the air just exactly as the person she was," Absher said. When the subject came up about her difficult life, "Miss Blue would always steer the conversation to the positive side." She'd always talk about how much she'd been blessed. "Jack was able to engage Miss Blue in a way that brought out the best from her. He was perfect for Miss Blue's personality," Absher said.

"In radio you have to believe a situation to see it," the *Post-Dispatch* said in a profile printed in 1975. "In person, Miss Blue's picture comes through as sincere as it does on radio. Having moved up from Mississippi at age 16, Miss Blue has retained the flavor and specificity of Southern speech. She has innate wisdom, and a deft humor that stands out against Carney's straight lines." It kept people coming back for more, but it couldn't last forever. She died of a brain tumor in 1983 at the age of sixty-nine. Her former listeners remembered her sweet voice, her wise advice, and the words "All is well."

# Dave Sinclair: Grandma's Car Dealer

The bad news in March 2009 was that more than thirteen million people were out of work. The unemployment rate stood at 8.5 percent and was headed to a high of 10 percent that October. But one local auto dealer fought the bad news by hiring twelve people, even though it didn't need them. The news that Dave Sinclair and his family of dealers were adding workers in the middle of a down economy at the end of the first decade of the century made the NBC *Nightly News with Brian Williams*. But around St. Louis, people saw it as just another good deed by a car sales guy known for years for shooting straight. "Life has been great. I was born and raised in Walnut Park," Sinclair told KSDK's Jennifer Blome during an interview about the hirings. "My wife was raised on Kingshighway and Thekla. We never thought we'd have anything. So it's been a great big wonderful life."

Much of that wonderful life came from Sinclair's years at the helm of a small local empire of car dealerships. He developed a reputation for honest dealings and hokey TV ads that made him a regional icon. In a business known for its crooks, everybody remembered him as the guy you told your grandmother to see about a car. He started his climb to the master of a local car dynasty after World War II, when he got a job carrying wet plaster up ladders at construction sites. Then, following in the footsteps of his father and grandfather, he went to work for the St. Louis Police Department.

Sinclair might have retired from the force if the pay had been good enough to cover the doctor's bill when one of his kids was injured in an accident in the 1950s. He borrowed the money to pay the bill from a relative who was a car salesman. Intrigued that the car-selling relative was so well off, Sinclair saved up days off and then spent eighteen days selling cars. He made more money in that time than he had in the previous six months. In 1956, he switched from patrolling a beat to catch crooks to patrolling a car lot to nab sales. Ford Motor Co. was so impressed by his success that it arranged in 1966 for him to have his own car dealership on South Kingshighway Boulevard.

In the late sixties, South Kingshighway was the place to go to buy a car. In 1969, there were twenty-one Kingshighway addresses from Chippewa to Arsenal where people could buy cars like Pontiacs, Cadillacs, Dodges, Lincolns, Oldsmobiles, and other brands. Sinclair worked to ensure that he got his share of business. He started a tradition by putting his seven kids to work and finding jobs for former cops. He became a pioneer in local advertising by buying his own thirty-second spots on KPLR-TV Channel 11. The first one showed white-gloved hands on a black background dealing cards that said, "For a great deal, come to Dave Sinclair." Later, he read his own copy behind a podium, as he did the rest of his life. Mostly, he told about the great deals and service at his place. He promised a free undercoat if anybody beat his deals. He'd let people know that if the car they bought wasn't right, he'd make it right. He'd end with the unchanging signoff, "Thank you, and here's my address." There was nothing slick about these ads, just a guy who looked like he just came from a Rotary meeting where he got his fifty-year membership award. But Sinclair connected with car buyers, and sales rolled in.

Sinclair kept things up into the new millennium and put his grandkids to work as he did his children. When recession hit at the end of the first decade of the twenty-first century, he and his kids responded by doubling advertising and lowering prices. After he died in September 2009, his family kept up the tradition that

Sinclair started. Today, the website of the David Sinclair Auto Group advertises ten different dealerships and two online used car operations. In 2016, the group celebrated its fiftieth anniversary with a sentimental ad combining pictures of Sinclair at various ages with an old commercial asking people to buy American products, even if his competitors sell them. "Hi. I'm David Sinclair, the all-car dealer from all over the place," Sinclair said as somber music played. "Thank you, and I'm not giving you any addresses on this one, but if you get lost looking for these guys, I sell American cars too." Dave Sinclair may be gone, but the promise remains that if the dealerships he started sell a car that isn't right, they'll make it right.

# Carl Hepp: High Art on Cable Access

It was the kind of conversation that would make Carl Hepp's day, about the weather, the news, or one of his favorite subjects, abortion. It stimulated Hepp and, just as importantly, cable access viewers, in St. Louis for about fifteen years during much of the 1980s and 1990s. But as Hepp prepared to hang up, the caller changed his tone and uttered the worse kind of language, known only to drunken sailors and writers of Facebook memes. Then a flustered Carl Hepp hit the cutout button and moved on to another caller.

It was one well-known feature of Hepp's Friday and Saturday night call-in program called *I'm Hepp*. At first, there was no delay. Out of nowhere, a caller would let loose with an obscenity, and Hepp would have to push the cutoff button. After a month or so, the calls were screened, but that

didn't stop everything. He might have a great conversation with someone, and then they would blurt out something crazy. When this happened, he just went to the next caller. His finger was constantly on the kill switch.

Hepp, a German expressionist artist, first got into cable access by helping a friend. After that, Hepp got his own program. A staunch Catholic, Hepp saw the program as a chance to speak out on issues important to Catholics, especially abortion. He also thought he could show off his artwork. He dressed as Frankenstein and as Father Time on New Year's Eve, but he had problems when he dressed as Santa with a beard made of cotton balls. As he sweated under the hot lights, the cotton balls got wet and fell apart. It was clear to all who watched that something was wrong. Nonetheless, Hepp did his best to keep going as if everything was fine. The next year, his sponsors bought him a decent beard that would stay fluffy throughout the program.

At times, Hepp would do a whole *I'm Hepp* program on a single subject. If he didn't like the calls he was getting, he would tell listeners, "If you're not going to participate properly, then you're going to listen to me talk." Then he wouldn't allow call-ins. He saved the worst censure of all for nights when every call was so much blather and codswallop. "St. Louis, you're dull, and you're boring," Hepp would pontificate. It's been years since Hepp went off the air, and nearly a decade since he died at seventy-four in 2007, but the words stick with his daughter Karen Hepp, who helped him with the program. "To this day, it's a haunting thought, what are you doing out there?" she said.

*I'm Hepp* was hardly enough for Carl Hepp's considerable talents in public access TV. So he also spent time on three smaller productions. One, *Carl Hepp's Amusements*, could have a crummy storyline—but one that came with catchy music and a plentitude of scenes of pavement and cars whizzing by. For an hour, viewers of that episode of *Carl Hepp's Amusements* who stayed with it watched traffic on Interstate 55 near the Anheuser-Busch Brewery and listened to the sound of Hepp whistling. Another time on the local cable access program, they saw nothing but shoes of people coming out of the old Globe Drug on Cherokee Street. "Are you trying to be amusing?" a police officer is heard saying. "You've hit that right on the head," Hepp said. There is no story about a St. Louis gendarme asking why Hepp aimed his camera at so many South

St. Louis doors and windows for a program called *Windows and Doors*. Hepp showed off his cooking skill in another program, *The Artist's Kitchen*. From time to time, he told viewers, he would be busy painting and would burn beans he was cooking. Callers would soon ask him, "Did you burn your beans today?" The shows may have been quirky, but that was Hepp's intent.

The show gained its share of listeners, but that wasn't enough for Carl Hepp. After a while, he wondered whether he was having an effect, including in promoting the pro-life message, Karen said. She assured him that if he'd helped one person decide not to have an abortion, he had reached his goal. He stayed, but he found it harder, as sponsors didn't always pay on time. There was no cost to get on cable access in the city, but there was one in St. Louis County. Eventually, he went off the air and returned to painting. Karen, a professional photographer, keeps his memory alive by preserving tapes of his programs and promoting his artwork. Karen thinks he'd be awesome today, with tablets, blogs, and tweets. On the other hand, he might still burn the beans.

# Fred Teutenberg: A Man and His Chicken

F red Teutenberg was too cheap, cheap to have a real actor appear on ads for Dirt Cheap Cigarettes and Beer stores. So he had fun, fun, doing spots with something that sorta kinda looked like a chicken.

Then Teutenberg would speak up. "Yes, it's cheap, but most of all, it's fun," he would say. "Best of all, the more she drinks, the better you look. I don't know about you, but I need all the help I can get." Then, poof! He assumed the physique of a body builder. In a typical ad, the chicken led shoppers in the Duck Dance, while in another, he broke out of a chicken egg before marching into a store. "Get all of your cheap beer, liquor, and wine and enjoy life on the cheap. Dirt Cheap," the chicken declares. With such ultra-tacky ads seen locally from the early 1990s to the end of the first decade of the twenty-first century, Teutenberg showed that Dirt Cheap Cigarettes and Beer was the place where people could feel free to hold on to their vices.

Teutenberg wasn't chicken about running the ads, nor was he only making jokes. "It was his nod to the fact that this was a far-from-pretentious party stop," said his daughter, attorney Elizabeth Ferrick. But Teutenberg, who led the Washington University debate club while he majored in political science, saw more than money in opening Dirt Cheap. His phrase "The last refuge of the persecuted smoker" was more than a slogan. Teutenberg didn't want his customers pushed around because they enjoyed a cheap smoke or

beer, and he didn't want big tobacco to muscle out the little guy, Ferrick said. He showed it in his commercials and as a primary spokesman whenever there were efforts to limit the use of tobacco. If the stuff's bad for you, Ferrick said, then so is too much sugar.

The name Teutenberg long has been familiar to St. Louisans. Back in 1812, a man named Franz Teutenberg started a pretzel shop not far from the present-day site of the south leg of the Gateway Arch. The family continued to run various businesses over the years, including a chain of cafeterias. With the company deeply in debt, Teutenberg closed the cafeterias in the early 1990s. From his research, he concluded that cigarette outlet stores were increasing in popularity all over the country. Teutenberg partnered with Paul Taylor, a friend from high school and college, to open the first Dirt Cheap store in Fenton in 1993, selling just tobacco products. Sales exploded, in no small part because of the Dirt Cheap chicken. Eventually, there were fourteen stores.

At the height of the stores, it was hard to be out in public with Teutenberg. "It was like you're out with a local celebrity," said Elizabeth Ferrick. At a Rams game, people asked him to sign their jerseys. Another daughter, Joannie Dalrymple, recalls being in contests, a Mardi Gras float, and a St. Patrick's Day float in a Mardi Gras celebration at the Lake of the Ozarks. Ferrick and Dalrymple played the chicken in some of those events. It seemed the stores would stay on forever. But then Teutenberg split with Taylor in 2009 for reasons neither disclosed. Teutenberg opened a new chain, Fred's Cheapo Depot, with stores in South County and downtown. A new chicken-less commercial featured Teutenberg mixing a martini while he was break dancing. The commercials he made were much on the mind of his customers when they learned of his death at the end of 2014. Hundreds upon hundreds came to his wake, many of them employees and former employees. He was buried with a pack of Kent Golden Lights and a bottle of Beefeaters Gin—his two favorite vices. To the end, he offered a last refuge for the smoker and a laugh whenever anyone thought of that "cheap, cheap, fun, fun" chicken.

# Elaine Viets: She Kills Us

For two decades, Elaine Viets covered the big stories in St. Louis. Like the guy who concreted his whole yard and painted it green because he was sick of cutting the grass. And the wedding she performed using ordination papers bought for a dollar through the mail. Not to mention the burning issue of the city's hoosiers. Then, in the mid-1990s, it seemed like she dropped dead. The truth is, she moved away and started writing books about people who dropped dead after being shot, poisoned, or inflicted with delightfully dastardly devices a good Catholic girl shouldn't imagine. But when she was growing up in St. Louis, Elaine Viets rebelled against one image of what a good Catholic girl should be.

"Back when I was growing up, nice Catholic girls were supposed to get married and have six kids," Viets said. Fortunately, nuns at St. Thomas Aquinas High School had a different idea and pointed her toward a writing career. Her parents objected. They wanted her to go to Fontbonne College (now Fontbonne University), which then was a proper "ladies" college. "I didn't want to be a lady, I wanted to be a newspaper reporter." When she decided to spend her first two years at the University of Missouri–St. Louis, her parents refused to pay for her education. So she worked her way through UMSL by proofreading medical books. There she fell in love with an UMSL instructor named Don

Crinklaw. Her parents came to the wedding but told her she could cancel the ceremony. "I said I'm getting married. And as far as I'm concerned, it's the smartest thing I ever did." Forty-five years later, they remain rapturously in love.

Viets finished her last two years at the University of Missouri School of Journalism and started at the *St. Louis Post-Dispatch* right after college. As a columnist, she brought laughs when she wrote about a makeup salesman at a department store. She invited readers to write in and say how bad their bosses were. One popular column reported that women were ogling a perfectly proportioned jogger who ran down South Kingshighway every morning.

Viets's column was one of the first places readers turned to when they picked up their papers. That changed, though, after her husband got a job in Washington, D.C. After they moved to Washington in 1994, the paper gave her a year to live and write in Washington and fly back at her own expense when she had to work in St. Louis. After twelve months, she asked her bosses for another year to continue the experiment. They refused, and that was the end of her job. Viets grabbed a position first as a syndicated columnist and then as a writer of mystery novels. About one hundred papers picked up her columns, but she got so busy writing the novels that she dropped the columns.

Her first four novels featured Francesca Vierling, a columnist for a St. Louis newspaper. Speculation exploded in the *Post-Dispatch* newsroom about which reporters she fictionalized for the book. In the next books, the Dead-End Job Series, she took jobs matching the work done by protagonist Helen Hawthorne. For research, Viets put aside her computer and took such menial jobs as a hotel maid, a telephone boiler room caller, and a sales person at a dog boutique.

Viets and her husband moved to Fort Lauderdale and were living the good life when a sudden health emergency arose that threatened to end everything. "I was misdiagnosed when I went to

the hospital. The neurologist on call said I was too young and fit to have a stroke, which is not true, and he said I should come back in a few days for a PET scan." Instead, she had six strokes, including a hemorrhagic stroke. She was in a coma for a week and underwent brain surgery. It took her a long time to figure out what had happened. She credits a surgeon who saved her life, her husband, and her friends for bringing her back. There was nothing easy about the therapy, and she had to learn to do everything again. She started writing after a year and pretty much recovered from her ordeal.

As of the summer of 2016, her byline was on thirty murder mysteries. She has frequently returned to her hometown to do such things as take the Medicolegal Death Investigators Training Course at St. Louis University and to do signings and give talks about her latest books. In her columns and her novels, Viets has seen the humor in situations and commits it to sentences and paragraphs meant to bring out the maximum numbers of snickers, giggles, and chortles in her readers. It makes for a great life, but it's not what her parents had in mind. The nuns would like it, though.

# Pete Parisi:
# TV for the Rejects

Holding a mike in front of the St. Louis Psychiatric Rehabilitation Center, Pete Parisi looked like he might be preparing for a hard-hitting TV report on mental illness. Until he opened his mouth. "We're at 5400 Arsenal Street, otherwise known as the nuthouse," he said, in front of the wrought iron fence around the hospital. In the background is the music of the widely criticized 1960s song about mental illness, "They're Coming to Take Me Away." Parisi then talks about a great dinner held at the hospital the night before. "It was a great dinner. It was a beautiful feast, like seven or eight courses and everything in it from soup to nuts."

It was outrageous, of course, but typical of what you could expect in the fifteen years the South Side resident was a favorite of local public access cable station viewers in the 1980s, 1990s, and the start of the new millennium. Those watching his show, *World Wide Magazine*, got used to seeing him get tossed from everything from the St. Louis victory party for Bill Clinton's re-election to the old VP Fair. But to that South Sider, it just made the show better. "When people cover over the camera, we love it, because it makes them look so bad," he said as he was told to leave. That happened a lot in the show, which was as much theater of the absurd as it was TV documentary. Many of the segments are still drawing viewers on YouTube.

Anything could happen in the unscripted segments of *World Wide Magazine*. "He was real direct and blunt about things. That's what made him interesting, I guess, because he would state the obvious," said Hill neighborhood resident Bruce Marren, a videographer who knew Parisi. "There was one [show] where he broke up with his girlfriend, and they were screaming and yelling at each other." With him would come such characters as Black Jesus and Vladimir Noskov as the Mad Russian. "It seemed he had that New York jerk kind of personality, but kind of likable," said Mike Algarda. Algarda worked at a TV repair shop where Parisi would bring in equipment for repair. He sometimes went to Parisi's apartment and watched him edit film. Morton Hill had mixed feelings about Parisi. Hill was the program director at Double Helix, which produced material for public access channels. As such, he saw Parisi as a pain because of the way he was always challenging FCC regulations. On the other hand, "He was a great guy."

A New Jersey native, Parisi started in 1969 at a Springfield, Massachusetts, radio station and became program manager of the old progressive radio station KADI in 1971. While Parisi was at KADI, the *Riverfront Times* noted in 2002, he played a cruel joke on his preschool niece and nephew that showed even then his lack of taste. On a visit home to New Jersey on Christmas Eve, he played them a cassette tape he'd produced. But they thought they were listening to a radio broadcast announcing that Santa Claus had died in a fiery plane crash. Niece and nephew broke down in tears.

Fired in 1983, he started work as a film editor at St. Louis's Channel 1. In 1986, he started showing stuff he'd shot on local public access channels. Audiences were kind as *World Wide Magazine* developed an audience, but he had one enemy. A diabetic, he never took care of himself. Doughnuts were a favorite food. His health started sliding, and it was harder for him to carry a camera. His production declined. In November 2001, while in Florida, he slipped into a diabetic coma. He died in January 2002 at the age of fifty-four.

In a 1997 interview with the *Post-Dispatch*, Parisi summed up the meaning of *World Wide Magazine* this way: "The whole show, if you really watch it, the whole show is based on unhappiness, sadness, society's rejects." Among those rejects, he said, was himself. He never made any money on *World Wide Magazine*. But if he was producing the same kind of material today, Algarda claims, he would be making plenty by showing it on YouTube. "Parisi today would probably be a multimillionaire," Algarda said. But if Parisi did, the program might change, because he would no longer be among the rejects.

# Mike "King of Credit" Stein: Comic by Accident

Three men holding what looks like vacuum cleaner hoses in their hands connected to backpacks dance in a smoky room in front of a couch, television, refrigerator, and washing machine. "There's something good at Union and Natural Bridge. Who you gonna call?" one sings. "Schweig Engel!" another answers. "We're going to give you a thousand dollars cash if Schweig Engel doesn't give you credit," the commercial says. "Now that's the Schweig Engel rental buster guarantee." The TV ad looked and sounded an awful lot like something out of the movie *Ghostbusters*, so much so that Columbia Pictures sent the local chain of appliance and furniture stores a cease and desist order to stop. Schweig Engel president Mike Stein pulled the commercials, but not before they brought in more business.

In more than five hundred radio and TV ads from 1981 to 2004, Stein lured in the laughs like somebody who's practiced comedy routines since kindergarten. But—surprise—before he did his first commercial, his sense of humor was as ho-hum as you'd expect from a former banker with a degree in accounting and finance from the University of Florida. Because that's what he was. The story of his transformation goes back to 1919, when the company was founded by members of the Schweig and Engel families, who were related by marriage. Stein, who is a descendant of those founders, claims the store was among the first sellers of radios and TVs in town and was an original sponsor of Cardinals radio broadcasts. Over time, it offered time payments for its products regardless of credit rating. While that put the company into a little-filled niche market, Schweig Engel faced serious problems at the start of the 1980s. Stein agreed to come up from his home in Florida to help out but only for a year.

Peeved that the ads provided by the company's ad agency weren't selling, Stein heeded the advice of a sales guy at a radio station that he should do his own commercials. So he started a commercial that was a parody of *Miami Vice*. "I really took on this persona because I wanted to do something that would stand out." The results were dramatic—too much so, actually. "We had to turn the ad off. It was so successful, we couldn't handle all the people who were coming in the store," he said. After taking a breath, Stein started the ads again, with astounding results. "In a matter of a year, we had almost doubled our business," he said. It was an accident, but people said he was a genius. His uncle, who had been in charge of the business, said Stein could run it. That, and meeting the woman he would marry, caused Stein to stick around St. Louis and take over.

Radio ads and commercials on KPLR kept bringing in more buyers. In one ad, customers were offered a free Mercedes Benz if they were turned down for credit. But things didn't always go well. Once, an employee's hair caught fire in the filming of an ad that called for a fire. Another time, Stein realized it was not a good idea to bring a horse into his store to film a commercial. Former world heavyweight boxing champion Joe Frazier and Cardinals player Willie McGee came by the store to meet him. "The commercials took on a life of their own. I was the King of Credit," he said. "It was really hard for me to go out to eat sometimes." When a fan approached him, he would sign a

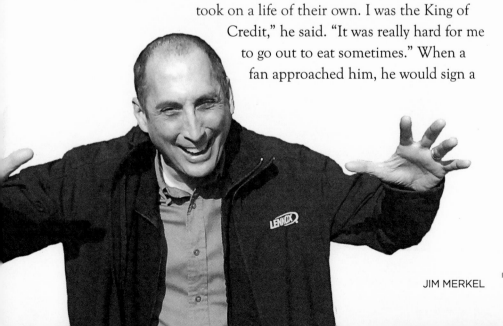

slick card showing himself as the King of Credit and hand it to that person. "We were asked to be in parades. I was every year in the Annie Malone Parade."

By 2004, Schweig Engel was rolling in cash. It had three stores and about $10 million in revenue. But it closed that year because of differences Stein had with his two partners. Stein got a management job with a heating and air conditioning company that is now Classic Aire. Looking back, he said Schweig Engel has received praise and awards for helping people get their credit back. "We were truly a second chance for a lot of people," he said. He had a specific market, and his ads reached it. "I really felt it could deliver my message of a second chance, of redemption." Looking back at his accidental transformation into a campy huckster, he said he didn't have a choice. He couldn't afford to hire an ad man himself, so he had to do it himself.

# Ray Hartmann:
# Twice in a Lifetime

When Ray Hartmann started a class newspaper in fourth grade, it was a sign of big things to come. Hartmann, it seems, has had a way of always putting out a new paper or magazine, even while he lent his liberal voice to KETC's *Donnybrook* every Thursday night for nearly thirty years. Two magazines he's led stand out for their must-read coverage of the Gateway City: the *Riverfront Times* and *St. Louis Magazine*.

With few breaks, Hartmann has led a publication almost continually since he started that elementary school paper and edited his high school newspaper at Parkway Central High School. At the University of Missouri in Columbia, he spent a year editing the *Campus Courier*, a student newspaper started by Republicans, and another two years editing Mizzou's main campus newspaper, the *Maneater*. After graduating in 1974, he was first a newspaper reporter and then wrote speeches for Governor Christopher "Kit" Bond. In 1977, he started a free paper called *Profile St. Louis*. It flopped, but a downtown paper he started was more successful: the *Riverfront Times*. The next year, he took on a partner, Mark Vittert, who later launched the *St. Louis Business Journal*.

Ray Hartmann views one of the earliest episodes of *Donnybrook*.

The *Riverfront Times* was pretty bad, Hartmann admits. But starting early in 1979, it offered something that did attract attention: free personal ads. "You could write anything you wanted," he said. "Anything" turned into lots of sexually explicit content from lots of people. "It was ahead of its time, sort of a chat room," he said. Over time, though, the paper became known for coverage of issues as well as the ads.

The *Riverfront Times,* for example, repeatedly questioned the large subsidies the VP Fair received from the St. Louis Convention and Visitors Commission. Then there was the paper's scoop in 1988 about a custody case involving William Busch, a son of August A. "Gussie" Busch Jr. It wouldn't have been a scoop if the *Post-Dispatch* hadn't killed a similar story by columnist Bill McClellan. *Post-Dispatch* managing editor David Lippman said his main concern was over the privacy of two children involved. Nonetheless, when the news came out, the St. Louis County prosecutor ordered William Busch to share custody with the mother. The *Post-Dispatch* then picked up the story. None of that would have happened without the *Riverfront Times.* "We broke a lot of stories," Hartmann said. "We weren't afraid of the power structure and the mainstream media." People grabbed the paper at newsstands to see articles like that. It was fat with ads. Seeing this, New Times Media bought the *RFT* in 1998 for an estimated $6 to $10 million.

Although they'd sold one magazine, Hartmann and Vittert still were in the publishing business. They acquired the name of the defunct *St. Louis Magazine* from the *St. Louis Business Journal* in 1994 and relaunched it in 1995. Today, *St. Louis Magazine* isn't into advocacy journalism, but it still provides quality coverage of St. Louis, going beyond the day-by-day grind of the *Post-Dispatch.* Hartmann's columns questioning the establishment line about the benefits of a new stadium to keep the NFL in St. Louis raised questions that other local media overlooked. So did the December 2015 article "Cornell McKay's Overturned Sentence

Calls Eyewitness Testimony into Question," about a young African American who was falsely identified as the killer of a woman in the Central West End in 2012.

"Ray Hartmann filled a need for St. Louis and allowed a lot of good, long-form, explanatory journalism to take place in St. Louis," said D. J. Wilson, a staff writer for the *Riverfront Times* from 1995 to 2003 who has written freelance articles for *St. Louis Magazine* since then. "Hartmann started a business, ran a business, sold the business, and shifted gears into a new business. His stance and his persona are his brand, and it is and was a popular one." Hartmann worked long hours for years to make the *Riverfront Times* a legitimate and worthwhile business, Wilson said. When Hartmann sold it, he shared some of the largesse with his workers, depending on their position and how long they'd worked for the *Riverfront Times*. Wilson's not positive, but he recalls that Hartmann gave him one thousand dollars. Hartmann didn't have to do that, Wilson said.

Hartmann credits his success to great editors and staffs and an ability to interact and connect with readers. Whatever it is, the *Riverfront Times* and *St. Louis Magazine* consistently produce the meaty journalism that historians will rely on a hundred years from now when they want to learn about life in the Gateway City around the start of the new millennium. It's more than a coincidence that he's done it twice.

# Amanda Doyle:
# She Ain't Boring

An early story about Lucy the Bear so excited little Amanda Doyle that she mailed it to *Highlights for Children*. The magazine rejected it. She suspects the illustration she sent along, showing a bloody bird in Lucy's mouth, may have been a factor in the rejection. But far from ending her wordsmithing pursuits, it made her bear down on her desire to spend a life writing. Since then, she has interviewed crazed fans outside

Graceland at Christmas and Indy 500 winner Dario Franchitti in his dressing room at the Indianapolis Motor Speedway while he changed clothes. She went "hogging" for enormous catfish with her bare hands on the Sangamon River in Illinois with "river rats" who do it for a living. She's dedicated to the proposition that if you're bored, you're boring. Amanda Doyle ain't boring. "Free spirit," "enthusiastic," or even "impulsive" are better ways to describe her.

Doyle's life of forming words into sentences started as

she grew up in Memphis and St. Petersburg–Tampa, Florida. In high school, her godmother, who spent her career as a reporter, suggested she investigate the University of Missouri School of Journalism. Doyle fell in love with the place when she visited it with her dad. "The reason I went into journalism was to give myself carte blanche to be nosy and to get into anywhere I wanted to go, even if I didn't know where those places were till I was there," she said. But at least once, her nosiness got her in trouble at the J-School. On assignment for the school's daily paper, the *Columbia Missourian,* Doyle and a classmate interviewed the comedian Sinbad. They excitedly accepted an offer to eat supper with Sinbad's entourage and to watch his show for free, even though it meant getting back to the newspaper's office well after deadline. "We waltzed back in to file so late, still on cloud nine, and were completely and instantly brought back to reality by our furious editors and copy desk staff," Doyle wrote. Their grade on the assignment was slashed. But Doyle doesn't care. To her, the experience was worth more than an "A."

Doyle kept collecting experiences after she graduated from Mizzou in 1994. She received her master's degree in environmental studies at Sangamon State University (now the University of Illinois–Springfield) in 1997 and then married Brian Marston, a St. Louis native she'd met at Columbia. The couple moved to Lafayette Square, where her life of extolling St. Louis began. "It's an easy place to make a splash. St. Louis people are just welcoming," she said. Doyle and Marston jumped into Metropolis St. Louis, a group formed to create and promote an environment in St. Louis that attracts and retains young people. She was the group's president around 2000, and left it around the middle of the decade. Her experience with Metropolis led her to co-host a weekly talk show on KDHX radio with fellow Metropolis member Thomas Crone. At any time, they might interview a mayor, an artist, a mover and a shaker, or someone truly odd. Doyle, who lives in the city's Tower Grove South neighborhood, recalls that it was live radio, frequently strange, but a lot of fun.

Metropolis also led Doyle to a job she had until recently. About 2000, she hooked onto a job at *Where Magazine,* a monthly publication for visitors to St. Louis. A favorite part of the position was writing stuff that brought people to off-the-beaten path neighborhoods. She found herself in unusual positions, like on the Goodyear blimp. Doyle's growing travel writing specialty led Reedy Press to ask her to write an eclectic guidebook to the area. *Finally, A Locally Produced Guidebook to St. Louis by and for St. Louisans, Neighborhood by Neighborhood* contains oddball recommendations for places around the St. Louis area. Reedy Press took note of the fact that Doyle is not only a travel writer but a mom. Her boy, Milo, is eight, and her daughter, Molly, is two. Those, Reedy told her, qualified her perfectly to write a book about the grandfather taking his grandkids on a trip to the Gateway Arch. So was born *To the Top! A Gateway Arch Story.* Her book *100 Things to Do in Saint Louis Before You Die* became the basis for *100 Things* guidebooks in nearly forty cities.

In 2016, she left *Where Magazine,* started a children's book for the Missouri History Museum, and began studying the history of civil rights in St. Louis since the 1700s. Doyle rarely knows the thing called "free time." But if she did, she'd visit a dozen coffee places, shop, poke around, and find stuff for her next book. Her life may be busy, but it's never boring.

# ENTERTAINERS

# Mickey Carroll: Gateway City Munchkin

The words forever made Mickey Carroll famous. "As coroner, I must observe, I thoroughly examined her, and she's not merely dead, she's most sincerely dead," he said in *The Wizard of Oz* in 1939. Born in 1919, the native St. Louisan had a multitude of opportunities to repeat those words and others as not just a Wizard of Oz Munchkin, but the one who provided the voice pronouncing the Wicked Witch most sincerely dead. He stood just over three feet in the movie, was fully grown at around four foot three, and always spoke in a boy's high-pitched voice. Curiously, the man who provided the coroner's voice in the movie came back to St. Louis in later years and sold tombstones.

Originally named Michael Finocchiaro, Carroll showed himself a ham from his earliest days living just north of downtown, at Eighth and O'Fallon Streets. "I would hang around the neighborhood carnivals and ask them to let me have a go at singing and dancing," he said. When he was ten, he started taking free tap dancing lessons at the Fox Theatre. He danced at the Muny in 1932 and danced the next year at a nightclub owned by Al Capone. Then he took off for Hollywood, where his roles included appearances in seven Spanky and Our Gang movies. Before long, he inked a contract with Metro-Goldwyn-Mayer and was going to school with Mickey Rooney and Judy Garland. In their free time, Carroll and Rooney went skating.

Carroll was back in St. Louis in 1938 when he got the call that changed his life. It was from Judy Garland, asking him to play the part of the coroner in *The Wizard of Oz*. He almost passed it up because the pay—$175 a week—wasn't enough to cover all his expenses. He changed his mind when Garland offered to put him up for the time the shooting would take. Everything was set, but an accident on the drive to Hollywood changed Carroll's role. The car he was riding in smashed into a parked truck. Doctors needed thirty-eight stitches to close cuts on his face. That wrecked his chances to play the coroner, but he did the voiceover declaring the witch "most sincerely dead." And he still played seven other roles. Garland always found time to spend with the Munchkins, Carroll said, but she clearly was overworked. He would get home at about 7 p.m., but Garland wouldn't come in until 1 a.m. She was made to take diet pills to keep from gaining weight, wouldn't eat, and often said she was dizzy.

The experience was a high point of Carroll's life, but hardly the only one. In Hollywood, he was George Murphy's roommate until Murphy started traveling. Then he learned that an actor named Ronald Reagan was looking for a roomie. Reagan moved in and soon showed he didn't know many recipes. As president, Reagan feasted on the most elegant meals prepared by the best chefs in the word. But as Mickey Carroll's roommate, he made nothing but liver and onions and hot dogs. "He was clean cut," Carroll recalled. "He kept a nice place. Nothing rowdy."

There were memories galore, but after a while he decided he'd had enough. Eventually, he moved back to St. Louis and sold granite and marble tombstones for his family's business, Standard Monument Co. He lived with his mother in north St. Louis County, took care of a nephew with cerebral palsy, and saw his twin sister of average height as much as possible. He never married, observing that he was a devout coward. But he had a family of thousands, made up of all who loved him for his role in *The Wizard of Oz.*

So many sent him letters and e-mails of appreciation that he gave up trying to respond to all of them. He chatted with fans from around the world at signings and Oz festivals. Charities counted on him to raise millions, especially the Special Olympics, Cancer for Kids, cerebral palsy, and programs for autistic children and breast cancer awareness. Locally, he always was willing to be grand marshal in a parade or master of ceremonies at a prom with an Oz theme. After he died in 2009, people thought he was most sincerely dead. But he came back figuratively, when family members sued a former caretaker for up to $249,000 she allegedly manipulated from him. After a jury rejected the claim, Mickey Carroll remained as he'd always been, the gentle Munchkin from St. Louis. Speaking about the reasons he returned to our town, he quoted Dorothy's words at the end of the movie. "'There's no place like home,' and that says it all for me," he said. "St. Louis is my home. I love the people here."

# Harry Fender: Mom Complex

B aby boomers who grew up in St. Louis usually don't recall the name Harry Fender, but more often than not they remember Captain 11's *Showboat*. One of several kiddie shows on local TV that featured local media folks in costume, this one showed an old guy wearing Mark Twain makeup, a handlebar mustache, and a captain's outfit and cap. Speaking in a deep voice that endeared him to kids and grownups alike, Captain 11 was known to keep the little ones tuned in with characters like Joe-Joe the Cook and occasional visits by the real-life Moe, Larry, and Curly Joe. The shows made for rich memories, but if that's all the boomers remember, they don't know much about Harry Fender.

The full story of Harry Fender began on July 2, 1896, when he was born in Frankfort, Indiana, the son of a telegraph operator and a traveling actress. It seemed Fender was destined to be a star when he made his first acting appearance when he was only seventeen months and two weeks old. After his parents divorced, Fender's mother brought him to St. Louis. There, he started singing for the Delmar Opera Company and the Park Opera Company. But St. Louis wasn't big enough for the blooming star, and he headed east for the big time.

Fender found acting jobs but little money and had to live in two-dollar-a-day tenements filled with lice in Pittsburgh, Atlantic City, and New York. So, just as America entered World War I, Harry Fender signed up for the navy and found himself as the juvenile lead in the *Great Lakes Revue* that toured the country raising money to fight the conflict. A fellow named Benny Kubelsky provided much of the comedy for the revue. Audiences later knew him as Jack Benny.

After the war, it looked like Fender would make it big when he was hired for one hundred dollars a week in *The Gaieties of*

*1919* with such big names as Ed Wynn and George Jessel. Within six years, producer Florenz Ziegfeld of Ziegfeld Follies fame was paying him fifteen hundred dollars a week. Everything seemed like it was coming up roses, but Fender suddenly started feeling an overwhelming sense of stage fright. He thought it might be a nervous breakdown, but it was something more. Nobody else seemed to mind, including Ziegfeld, who soon offered him the lead male role in a new musical called *Show Boat.* Ziegfeld wrote to him that it was a once-in-a-lifetime opportunity that he shouldn't throw away.

But Fender did turn the offer down and ran first to Europe and then to Palm Springs. He nixed new offers and eventually returned to St. Louis, where a doctor tried to figure out what was wrong with him. His agent showered him with offers, but Fender turned his back on all that and signed up with the St. Louis Police Department. Where once he was making $1,500 a week, he was now making $155 a month. But Harry Fender didn't care. As the head of the police gambling squad, he was involved in 150 raids. The governor of Missouri dispatched him to Kansas City to investigate the mobs because people didn't know him there. Playing a gangster from Ohio may have been the role of a lifetime for the former Broadway star. He often went out with an automatic taped to his leg. "It was murder pulling that tape off every night," Fender said.

Fender went back to the public after he retired from the police force in 1945. He did features for KWK radio and worked for KXOK and KMOX. He accepted a role in a revue called *A Toast to the Twenties* that played at the Chase Park Plaza. But when his old fear of acting reappeared, he went back to a psychiatrist to find out why. The verdict: a mother complex. "It was the doctor's theory that I was obsessed with a fear of not doing well enough to please my mother," he said.

Working with that knowledge, Fender pleased the kiddies in the 1960s with his rendition of a waterborne captain. He followed this as a regular on KMOX's Jack Carney show. When Fender finished telling Carney's 105,000 listeners about old times on Broadway, Carney would pose the question: "How old are ya, Harry?" Fender laughed and said, "Isn't he terrible, folks?" The answer to that question, when Fender died in 1995, was ninety-eight. Fender had lived a full life in three careers, and Captain 11 was just a small part of it.

# Joe Besser: The Stooge from St. Louis

Y ou've heard about the kid who wanted to run away to the circus? Joe Besser not only dreamed of doing it, he actually did it, at the age of twelve. If you think running away from home made him a stooge, you're right. For two years during the 1950s, he played beside Larry Fine and Moe Howard as one of the Three Stooges. His work with the Three Stooges represented just a small part of his work over a comedy career that lasted two-thirds of a century. He kept them laughing in more than 40 motion picture roles, 250 television appearances, a radio show, a short subject series, plus numerous appearances on Broadway. He performed with such acting giants as Abbott and Costello, Joey Bishop, Jackie Gleason, Bing Crosby, Debbie Reynolds, Robert Wagner, Jerry Lewis, Sammy Davis Jr., and Marilyn Monroe. But his role as a Stooge overshadowed all else.

Besser first trained for that work as one of eleven children (two of whom died in childbirth) of two poverty-stricken Jewish immigrants. Morris Besser came from Russia, Fanny from Poland. They emigrated to New York in 1895, where Morris worked as a baker, then hopscotched to Cincinnati and St. Louis, where Joe was born on August 12, 1907. For the first five years of their life, the Bessers were stuffed in a two-story duplex. Joe slept on a couch in the dining room. His older brother Manny made things a bit less cramped when he left around the time Joe was born to join the Buffalo Bill Traveling Show. As he grew, Besser wanted to be like his big brother.

His break came when he fell in love with a traveling circus called the Barnes Carnival and one of its magicians, named Howard Thurston. After Thurston performed in St. Louis, Joe snuck into a train car in Thurston's circus bound for Detroit. Thurston decided that anyone who wanted to be with him that badly should stay. He contacted Joe's parents, who gave their blessing. So began a life of making 'em laugh.

Besser rubbed shoulders with the likes of Cab Calloway, Sophie Tucker, and Al Jolson as he rose through the ranks of the laugh makers. When he did get home to see the family, he gave everybody fits. In an obituary published after Besser died at eighty in 1988, his sister Gertrude Tobias of University City said he could be a pest and a show-off. "He would do card tricks when we had dates over. Sometimes we had to throw him out of the house. He was very good-natured. He never did anything mean. He was full of fun." In 1928, he was smitten by a dancer in his show, Erna Kay Kretschmer. "Not another entertainer!" her mother said when she brought him home. No matter. Joe and Erna said their vows in 1932, the day before Besser appeared in a show in Baltimore. That year, he first met the Three Stooges.

Tragedy made Besser a Stooge, after Shemp Howard had a fatal heart attack in Chicago two days before Thanksgiving 1955. Besser was offered the job and agreed with one proviso: Moe or Larry couldn't inflict the kind of physical harm that Curly and Shemp had received. Moe and Larry agreed, and Larry said he'd take the punches. But Besser was still on the receiving end of some hits. With Besser on board, the Three Stooges did sixteen fifteen-and-a-half- to seventeen-minute films for Columbia Pictures in 1956–57. In A Merry Mix-up, confusion reigns when three sets of identical triplets separated during the war (all looking like the Three Stooges) suddenly encounter each other. They face three cannibalistic Amazon alien women on the planet Sunev (Venus spelled backwards) in Space Ship Sappy, while Joe dreams that the Stooges' sister was reincarnated as a horse in Hoofs and Goofs. When they finished making the films, Columbia Pictures told them their services were no longer needed. Besser could have gone on the road with Moe and Larry, but he wanted to stay close to his wife, who had just had a heart attack. The Three Stooges went on with a burlesque comic named Joe DeRita, who was renamed Curly Joe.

Besser remained in the funny business for more than twenty-five years after he left the Three Stooges. He was present in 1983 when the Three Stooges belatedly received a star on the Hollywood Walk of Fame. It bothered him sometimes that his work with the Three Stooges overshadowed some other great accomplishments in his career. But he grew to accept it. To him, his time with the Three Stooges was his happiest period in show business.

# Davey Bold: A Nose for Comedy

D avey Bold's wildly oversized nose was impressive enough to warrant its use in a nickname. It extended from his face like Gibraltar and was such a hallmark that people knew him as Davey "Nose" Bold. The pianist and comic entertained countless St. Louis audiences from the 1940s into the 1960s. In 1989, eleven years after Bold died of a heart attack, *Post-Dispatch* reporter Dick Richmond wrote that he was the only one who did comedy on a regular basis in St. Louis after the city's Grand Burlesque closed in 1964. Bold once quieted a heckler by asking his hometown and then remarking, "My father used to bum around your hometown. You know, you may be my brother."

Bold joked that his first job was as a bartender in a hardware store in his hometown of Chicago. He snatched the hardware store job and was told to sell Sterno to drunks. It was a solid form of alcohol, but drunks got a buzz out of it. "It was a dime a can," he quipped. "I wasn't even allowed to make change." He kept looking and hooked a job as a piano player at a sleazy bar for fifteen dollars a week, from 8 p.m. until morning. He quit in six months to make more money and started moving up. After a few years, he mixed in humor. He served as a straight man to a comedian but started doing his own routines when he discovered that making people laugh helped his bottom line. After a while, he got offers to do stand-up comedy for five hundred to one thousand dollars a week.

In the 1940s, he played off and on for three years at Johnny Perkins' Palladium in East St. Louis. In St. Louis, he played at the Port Plaza Lounge and the Claridge Hotel. He and his wife decided they liked St. Louis and that their daughter would benefit from the special education available here. So they moved here, and he grabbed a job with the Celebrity Club. While he was in St. Louis, Bold played at places like Gaslight Square and the Playgirl Club. He

was in the Municipal Opera's production of *Molly Darling* while he was in St. Louis, appeared in the movie *The Hoodlum Priest*, and was a regular on local TV programs. "I used to introduce the programs, tell jokes, make fun of the commercials," he said, discussing *Ellery Queen* and *Star Showcase*, two programs he did in the early days of TV. "The shows had pretty good ratings too," he said, adding, "Of course, I was opposite public service programs."

Bold joyed in entertaining the crowds with the 1937 Guy Lombardo hit "It Looks Like Rain in Cherry Blossom Lane." He often appeared with such big names as Joey Bishop, Henny Youngman, Rowan and Martin, and Jimmy Durante. He talked about his nozzle on stage until a comic known everywhere for his nose brought him low. "Hey, folks, this is Davey 'Nose' Bold," he once told an audience. Little did he know that behind him was Durante and his well-known schnoz. Durante spoke up, "Hey, dat man is an imposter." As Bold perspired, Durante took over. "Get off, get off," Durante said. "I'm the only nose." People still used the middle name after that, but he just introduced himself as Davey Bold.

Bold had better luck when he was called on at the last minute to talk to aeronautical engineers at the old McDonnell Aircraft

Corporation of St. Louis. McDonnell, which made the first space capsules, had a commitment from Wernher von Braun, the German developer of key American rockets, including the one that took the first Apollo astronauts to the moon. But when von Braun couldn't make it, the company turned to Bold. Bold knew nothing about aeronautics, but he knew plenty about talking gobbledygook. After ten minutes or so, the flummoxed McDonnell workers realized that Bold had engineered a fast one on them.

Bold moved to Omaha in the 1960s and often entertained in Minneapolis, but he maintained his connection with St. Louis by making occasional appearances here. He was often the butt of his own jokes. "I have such bad luck," he grumbled, "that when I telephone Dial-a-Prayer, they hang up." He spoke of having doctor jokes ready when a doctor was in the audience and plumber jokes when a plumber came in. His nose may not have measured up to the schnoz on Jimmy Durante, but it still was awesome to behold.

# Marlin Perkins: TV's First Man of Animals

**W**hen a poisonous cottonmouth decided to chomp down on the curator of the St. Louis Zoo in 1928, he calmly took notes about how his body and mind reacted to the serpent's venom. When a Gaboon viper bit the curator again two months later, his assistant likely saved his life by sucking the wound, in the best Boy Scout tradition. For R. Marlin Perkins, it set a pattern of fearless dedication to animals at zoos in Buffalo, Chicago, and St. Louis and for viewers of his pioneering animal

television broadcasts. He could teach people to love animals because he loved them first.

Almost from the time Perkins was born in 1905, he was keeping animals. He started as a laborer at the St. Louis Zoo in 1926 and soon was curator of the reptile house. "I was in charge of the reptile house for eleven glorious years. We had two huge pythons," he said in 1970. He had to force-feed one, which meant extra work. "I used to stuff a length of hose with ground-up rabbit and horse meat and lubricate the end with a solution of slippery elm." As reptile house keeper, he saw the zoo's reptile collection expand from six to five hundred by the time he became director of the New York Zoological Gardens in Buffalo, New York, in 1938. Another job change came in 1944, when he became director of the Lincoln Park Zoo in Chicago. It was the dawn of television broadcasting, and he did his part to be one of the first animal broadcasters, on WBKB in Chicago. For his first show, he set a pulsating bullfrog on a desk and demonstrated how its throat pumped air into its lungs.

The shows were hardly flashy, but they did lead to bigger things. In 1950, he became host of *Zoo Parade*, on the NBC Television Network. Keepers brought animals to the basement of the Lincoln Park Zoo's reptile house, where filming took place. Soon *Zoo Parade* went on the road to such locales as Nairobi National Park and Mount Kilimanjaro. In the Amazon, he captured footage of a Yagua Indian shooting a ten-inch dart dipped in muscle poison through a blowgun to kill his prey. When he did that, Perkins brought the show closer to the feel of nature programs today.

NBC canceled *Zoo Parade* in 1957, but Perkins kept traveling. In 1960, he ventured with Sir Edmund Hillary, one of the first two

men to climb Mount Everest, on an expedition to the Himalayas to find whether there really was an Abominable Snowman. He concluded that the huge tracks in the snow attributed to the snowman actually were fox tracks that grew much bigger when they melted. Perkins returned to the Lincoln Park Zoo, and in 1962 he was offered a job as director of the St. Louis Zoo. He accepted the position, and the next year he returned as host of a new NBC animal program, *Mutual of Omaha's Wild Kingdom*.

As St. Louis Zoo director, Perkins did what he could to make sure keepers lavished the animals with loving care. "It's very important that keepers be close friends with their charges," he said. "A friend can trim their claws, work on their teeth, or give them medicine, but the animals would be terrified of strangers. Anyway, animals feel better if they know they are wanted." He started a zoo nursery, the Children's Zoo, and the Zoo Line Railroad, and put more emphasis on education. He fenced in the zoo to protect the animals and to stop the occasional drunk who decided to wrestle alligators. In spite of those innovations, some thought his visits to Alaska, the Kalahari, and other exotic locales for *Wild Kingdom* took him away from his day job at the St. Louis Zoo. He survived that talk, just as he survived claims that *Zoo Parade* was eating into his time as director of the Lincoln Park Zoo.

But Perkins couldn't survive the march of time. In 1970, he retired as director of the St. Louis Zoo and was named director emeritus. He hosted *Wild Kingdom* until 1985, the year before he died. By that time, he had long since given up correcting people who said they saw him on TV being bitten by a timber rattlesnake. As Snopes vouches, the rattler bit him during rehearsal, while he was preparing to demonstrate how to extract snake venom.

# Phyllis Diller: Funny Lady

Phyllis Diller grew up in Ohio and probably never heard about a St. Louis hoosier before she moved to Webster Groves in the 1960s. But her monologues sounded like the latest gossip from a house on a Jefferson County back road with a rusted 1949 Ford pickup on blocks out front. The neighbor—"Mrs. Clean"— always bragged how she could eat off her kitchen floor, Diller told her audiences. "You can eat off my kitchen floor. Mustard, ketchup, baked beans." Her mouth opened wide as she let loose with her ever-ready cackle. "The other night, Fang—that's my husband, the idiot—he said, 'It's certainly not the stew my mother used to make.' I said, 'Heavens no, that's custard pie.'" Wherever she went, and in all of her pictures, her blonde hair stood up like she'd just been shocked, and her eyes and mouth stayed wide open. After she died in 2012, it was easy to think she lived a laugh. But she had a darker side that most didn't know.

Born in 1917 as Phyllis Driver, she grew up in Lima, Ohio. A skilled pianist, she studied at Sherwood Conservatory of Music in Chicago and transferred to Bluffton College near her home. There she met and married Sherwood Diller. To provide for her children and five kids, she found work writing advertising copy. She was a natural. Friends and her husband told her she had a way of making people chuckle. They urged her to try comedy.

Encouraged, she started a two-week stint at San Francisco's Purple Onion in 1955. The temporary gig lasted two years. Soon she was in demand on the road and for television programs like *Tonight Starring Jack Paar* and Bob Hope specials. As her fame grew, she felt a need for a central location where she could live between gigs. St. Louis seemed a good choice. Her husband's sister and mother lived in an apartment over the old Eagle Drug at Vandeventer Avenue and Shaw Boulevard. Her youngest children, Stephanie and Perry, stayed there while she, her husband, and their older children traveled. In 1962, Diller bought an eleven-room pink stucco colonial house on Mason Avenue in Webster Groves.

It should have been a dream home, but it wasn't. Suffering from schizophrenia, her daughter Sally was institutionalized after she wouldn't respond to treatment. Meanwhile, Diller's relationship with her husband deteriorated. He was mentally ill, prone to anxiety attacks, subject to tirades, often wouldn't leave the house, and sometimes refused to bathe. But the house did offer Diller and her family a sense of normality while she traveled. When she was in town, Diller appeared on local venues like TV's *Charlotte Peters Show*. Into this world came Patricia Corrigan, a classmate and friend of one of Diller's daughters, Stephanie Diller. Corrigan, a former *Post-Dispatch* reporter who is now an author living in San Francisco, recalls looking through closets in the family's basement stuffed with sack dresses Diller wore on stage, wig trees, feather boas, two pipe organs, a piano, drums, and horns.

The friends separated when Diller moved her family to Los Angeles in 1965. Diller divorced her husband. Her marriage to actor Warde Donovan the same year also ended in divorce. In the 1960s, she had her own television show and starred in movies from the serious *Splendor in the Grass* to the comedies *Boy, Did I Get a Wrong Number* and *Eight on the Lam*.

From 1972 to 1982, she played piano seventy-five times with symphony orchestras. She always remembered St. Louis with fondness. "Gaslight Square and the Crystal Palace. Those were great times," she said. She had pleasant memories of returning to St. Louis to perform in *The Wizard of Oz* and *Cinderella* at the Muny. "What a lovely park, what a lovely town."

Diller kept going with comedy appearances and TV shows until she arranged a farewell standup performance in 2002. She was still skewering Fang, his family, and most of all, herself. Off camera, she was all elegance. "I always said I would like to become a gracious lady. Like be known for kindness," she said in a documentary made of the final show. But in that show, she was the picture of the rejected housewife. "The house is full of bugs, and I could care less," she bellowed, as she delivered one zinger after another, pacing throughout the show. "My archenemy is that little goody two shoes, Martha Stewart." Bang. "The problem is Fang wants everything to taste like mother used to make it." Pause. "Where in the hell can I buy fresh buffalo meat?" Pow. The crowd chortled throughout, as she went out with a bang.

# Slim Cox: Down Home on the South Side

For most girls, the end of school on Friday means the start of a weekend relaxing and hanging out with friends. But for Sharon Hardcastle, it meant the start of another weekend motoring hundreds of miles from one church singing engagement to another as a child of Almus "Slim" and Zella Mae Cox. "It was very exciting and sometimes very tiring," said Hardcastle, recalling those days on the road with her family. "I've been singing ever since I can remember." Another daughter, Brenda Chitty, said, "It was like spinning in a circle around and around." Indeed, music defined the family. "They were always singing, and they were always on the radio," Hardcastle said.

When they sang, Slim and Zella Mae brought the down-home gospel sound of two people who grew up dirt poor in Arkansas. Born in Datto, Arkansas, in 1927, Slim never forgot the country or the poverty of his youth. After he was born on May 27, 1927, his parents couldn't afford to pay the doctor, so they gave him three dozen eggs and a red rooster. When he was fourteen, he bought himself a piano for $7.50 and taught himself how to play. He honed his style playing in bands and then with Zella Mae after they married in 1948. When Zella Mae was born on October 23, 1930, in Mammoth Springs, Arkansas, her parents didn't have to give up three dozen eggs. Her father, a Pentecostal preacher, delivered her. Slim maintained he found out he really loved Zella Mae when he discovered she could pick 360 pounds of cotton a day. After they married, they sang on small radio stations in northern Arkansas and southern Missouri. They continued performing on the radio after he moved to Wellston in the late 1950s and worked for Schweig Engel Furniture. After twelve years at Schweig Engel, Cox started his furniture company at 2831 Chippewa Street.

In the morning before school, the Coxes recorded a fifteen-minute show at home. Cox then took the tape to KXEN Radio. They also recorded at least sixteen albums and spent weekends driving to singing engagements as far away as Nashville on an old Greyhound bus. Slim and Zella Mae and their four kids would take off in a car on Friday night and get back late Sunday night. On a busy weekend, they'd play at services on Friday night, Saturday morning and Saturday night, and Sunday morning and Sunday night. Early in the 1970s, they got an old Greyhound bus. Hardcastle's husband went along and shared the driving duties with Slim. They'd motor well into the night before stopping early in the morning for a little sleep.

Sharon Hardcastle and her husband, DeWayne Hardcastle, traveled with the Coxes from 1970 to 1976. "He was just a natural showman," DeWayne Hardcastle declared. "He just had the gift of gab." He contends Cox had a gifted presentation that people enjoyed. Everything Cox related he'd experienced, he contended. "There was nothing fake about him. He was just Slim." Other musicians have one persona on stage and another off, he said. Slim Cox was always the same.

After about fifteen years, the Coxes sold their bus and concentrated on St. Louis, particularly work on the radio and television stations of Larry Rice's New Life Evangelistic Center. Slim kept playing his lively country style of piano. "That's why Slim and Zella Mae can get up in those telethons and get the phones ringing," Slim said, in the booming voice that watchers of the telethons and other programs on the stations knew well. He didn't mind that he never had a lesson and never learned how to read notes. It was more important that he play country gospel like his favorites, Jerry Lee Lewis, Jimmy Swaggart, and country gospel musician Howard Goodman. If he just read the notes in a service, everybody in church would fall asleep, Cox said. People knew about the music far beyond the range of Larry Rice's radio and TV stations. They heard it on stations as far away as Poland, Australia,

Denmark, Canada, and England, and in numerous states in the United States. "It makes me feel thrilled to know we're getting to people," Slim said.

As an octogenarian, Slim loved to talk about the old days, whenever people came into his furniture store. In the years before Slim died in 2012 and Zella Mae followed in 2014, the two would lead people to their radio and recording studio in the back of their store and break out in the kind of gospel songs listeners ate up on down-home radio. "He just loved having people coming in. He'd get back there and play the piano," said Sharon Hardcastle. They kept spreading the gospel and enjoyed life in the city, but they remained country folks from Arkansas.

# Stan Kann: Vacuum Man

For years, Stan Kann kept TV audiences roaring with seemingly bumbling efforts to demonstrate how old vacuum cleaners and other gizmos worked. But the first time he did it on *The Tonight Show,* he was such a klutz that Johnny Carson brought him back again and again. The sight had Johnny Carson and his audience roaring with laughter. Kann nervously fidgeted as he tried to demonstrate his collection of ancient vacuum cleaners. But the more he tried, the more things went wrong. The more he pumped the nineteenth-century machines, the more they left grime on the floor.

It wasn't just an act for Kann, who grew up in St. Louis, moved to Hollywood in 1975, and moved back to spend the last decade of his life on Federer Place on the South Side. "He could play any music," longtime friend Judy Brilliante told a reporter for the *South Side Journal* after he died in 2008 at the age of eighty-three. "He knew it in his head. He had it. But if you asked him where he parked his car, forget it." Ed Schroeder, director of volunteer services at the Fabulous Fox, said that was the way it was when Kann played at the theater from 1999 to the night before he died. Kann needed a space to park his car, an organ to play his music, and an abundant supply of napkins to wipe up all the coffee he spilled.

That's pretty much how Kann kept coming back to Johnny Carson after that first fumble-filled appearance in 1965 turned into a regular gig. Altogether, he made seventy-seven guest appearances on Carson's show, eighty-nine on the old *Mike Douglas Show,* and thirty-two on the *Merv Griffin Show.* Kann had a perfect comedic sense, especially when Carson played straight man. He had a syndicated show in Canada for three years, was a character in two situation comedies, and played the organ as background for the television series *M\*A\*S\*H.* But he spent his younger years on Washington Avenue, collecting vacuum cleaners and honing his musical talents. As he built his reputation locally, he played the organ at the old Fox Theatre and at Ruggeri's Restaurant from 1953 to 1975. The local older set will remember him as co-host of TV's *The Noon Show* with Marty Bronson and as a regular on the *Charlotte Peters Show*.

It was through those appearances that he made friends with slapstick comedian Phyllis Diller, who lived in Webster Groves at the time. Bemused by Kann's collection of more than a hundred old vacuums, she persuaded Carson to have him on his show. That's where the miscues began. As Kann told the old *South Side Journal*, he was waiting to go on when he went through the wrong door, down a fire escape and then out into the street. By the time he talked his way back to where he was supposed to be, he was beside himself. To the delight of his audience, he was so flustered on camera that everything went wrong.

Tom Gasko, a longtime friend of Kann's and the curator of the Vacuum Cleaner Museum and Factory Outlet in St. James, said Kann told him another factor made Kann look like he didn't know what he was doing during his first time on with Johnny Carson. Kann took the vacuums apart to ship them to New York. Not realizing that Kann would want to demonstrate them, the union workers in the prop department assembled them just enough to stand them within view of a camera. When he actually pushed one across a rug, the handle fell off. Trying to keep things going, he nonchalantly grabbed another, which also fell apart, and then another.

Kann loved to joke with his neighbors on Federer Place. "He just had a tremendous sense of humor," neighbor Bernice Mueller said after he died. At night when she and her husband, Norman, sat on their porch, Kann would join them. "He could come out with some doozy sayings sometimes, kind of twist his words around. He was really funny." The vacuum cleaners looked strange, Bernice Mueller said. But, she said, "He helped us by being such a good neighbor and friend. He had a heart as big as himself."

# Miles Davis: Deep Freeze of Cool

Miles Davis came from a musical family—so good, the story went, that members of the family played classical music even as slaves before emancipation. He wrote in his autobiography that a deadly tornado that roared through St. Louis a year after he was born in 1926 in Alton may have brought the power to his legendary trumpet playing. "Maybe that's why I have such a bad temper sometimes; that tornado left some of its violent creativity in me," he wrote. He turned from the church and its spirituals and toward the blues at an early age. He was always changing his style and widening the meaning of jazz. In the last half of the twentieth century, he was the King of Cool, the most influential jazz player of his generation. Yet he never escaped the memory of the racism he experienced in his own childhood.

The bloody East St. Louis race riots of 1917 were nine years in the past when Davis was born, the son of a well-to-do dental surgeon who brought him from Alton to East St. Louis. He always heard stories of the way African Americans were massacred for taking the jobs of white people who worked at East St. Louis packinghouses. He disappointed his mother when he didn't play the violin. Instead, his father gave him a trumpet for his thirteenth birthday. From then on, he wouldn't put it down. He soon played professionally on both sides of the Mississippi. In 1944, when he was eighteen, the trumpet player in Billy Eckstine's band got sick, and Davis filled in. Suddenly, he was a coworker with

four young pioneers of bebop jazz: Dizzy Gillespie, Charlie Parker, Art Blakey, and Sarah Vaughn. He went back to New York with Eckstine and studied classical music at the Juilliard music school during the day while performing jazz at night. He quit Juilliard to spend all his time at jazz clubs. His father reluctantly agreed and offered this advice: "Miles, you hear that bird outside the window? He's a mockingbird. He don't have a sound of his own. He copies everybody's sound, and you don't want to do that. You want to be your own man." Heeding those words, Davis joined Parker's quintet in 1945 and made his first recording as a bandleader in 1947.

From then on, Davis was known for the innovations he brought to jazz. In 1949 and 1950, he brought a nine-piece band into a studio to record *Birth of the Cool.* In the late 1960s, he teamed up with such leading jazz and rock musicians as Chick Corea, guitarist John McLaughlin, bassist Harvey Brooks, bass clarinetist Bennie Maupin, and percussionist Jack DeJohnette in such smash hit albums as *Filles de Kilimanjaro, In a Silent Way,* and *Bitches Brew. Bitches Brew* represented an experimental foray into fusion. It wasn't as famous as *Kind of Blue,* but it was very successful and served as an example of the uniqueness his father encouraged. At the top of his career, he played to sold-out audiences but pulled back after both of his ankles were broken when he fell asleep at the wheel of his Lamborghini in 1972 and crashed it into a divider. After that, he spent more of his time recording in the style of *Bitches Brew*. In 1975, a hip ailment forced him to stop recording and making concert appearances. Encouraged by his new wife, actress Cicely Tyson, he renewed his career at the start of the 1980s. He kept winning awards and recording new albums. He published his autobiography and worked with Brooklyn rapper Easy Mo Bee in *Doo Bop*, which mixed hip-hop, doo-wop, and bebop.

Davis's music could be sad and moody, matching his own character. "Miles Davis was the Dark Angel of Jazz," wrote biographer Vincent Bessières. Interviewers wondered if he would lash out or be a charmer. It depended on the day. When he didn't like somebody, he said so. He ended a heroin addiction in 1954 but still struggled with cocaine. Sometimes he turned his back on his audiences while he was playing and walked off stage when he didn't solo. But there was another side of his volatile, sensitive personality, noted by the writer of his biography on the website of the Rock & Roll Hall of Fame: "He possessed one of the most gifted and curious minds in music history, and compromise was not in his blood." He might have kept changing and influencing jazz had he not died in 1991 at the age of sixty-five. As it was, he changed the music form with all the force of the tornado that rammed its way through St. Louis in 1927.

# Charlotte Peters: The First Lady of St. Louis TV—and Corn

I t wasn't the kind of outfit for performers who prized their dignity, but dignified was the last word anyone would use to describe Charlotte Peters. Wearing a black tutu over a black one-piece swimsuit and a crown on her head, she played a sort-of ballerina, while she sang a song meant to mine her audience for every laugh she could get. "Get a load of me, I'm galloping around like a gazelle, making like a swell,

showing them what class is," she said, not long before the tutu "accidentally" dropped off. She knew how to clown around, and St. Louisans loved her for it. Throughout the 1950s and 1960s, she was the queen of local TV, as the hostess of a variety show called the *Charlotte Peters Show.*

It seemed Charlotte Peters had a PhD in grabbing audiences. In fact, her education ended after the eighth grade. She began life in 1912 as Charlotte Bert Wiederman and grew up in a second-floor apartment on Lafitte Avenue in St. Louis. Home was across the street from her father's favorite tavern. Early on, she danced on top of the bar as a musician banged on the keys of the tavern's piano.

Childhood ended after Charlotte graduated from grade school and was sent out to find work. She held a variety of jobs, including supervising women putting handles on golf clubs. At twenty-two, she married a wholesale dress company employee named Willie Peters and settled into the life of what they called back then a "housewife." She had two kids, Patricia and Mike. Mike grew up to be a political cartoonist and the creator of the comic strip *Mother Goose & Grimm*. A 1956 *Post-Dispatch* article noted that even then Mike Peters had the requisite sense of humor for such work. "Charlotte: 'Mike, did you take a bath?' Mike: 'Why, is one missing?'"

Back then, women stayed housewives. But not Charlotte Peters. "Her home and family mean everything to her," the 1956 *Post-Dispatch* article said. But, the paper said, ". . . the show business itch, one of the least curable maladies known, was always there, all through the diapers and detergent days." In the late 1940s, she auditioned in the KSD-TV (now KSDK) Amateur Contest. She won with the song "Won't You Come Home, Bill Bailey" and soon signed as a regular on a daytime show called *To the Ladies*, hosted by a man named Russ Severin. When he left for a job out in Los Angeles in 1952, KSD tapped Peters to replace him. As her audience skyrocketed, KTVI hired her away.

"Like many showpeople she cries easily, she has the quick tears. Her laugh startles passersby for blocks around," John Keasler noted. With St. Patrick's Day nearing, she persuaded the police chief to send out dozens of Irish cops as guests. When she had to quiz a hawker of camel saddles, she made another call to the St. Louis Zoo. "Can I borrow a camel?" she asked. "I don't think so," the befuddled folks at the zoo said.

Mid Day Fun!

**CHARLOTTE PETERS**

entertains with music, guests and stunts—weekdays

**12 noon**

**KSD-TV** Channel **5**

It was easy to believe Charlotte Peters always would be on St. Louis TV. But her reign came to an end when KTVI fired her after she signed off on July 10, 1970. Peters told the *Globe-Democrat* that her "usual outspokenness" cost her her job. She claimed that the bosses fired her because that day she criticized the presence in Forest Park of an event of the radical group the Youth International Party, or the Yippees. "They said they were going to have LSD and I urged my audience to write or call the mayor and board of aldermen to prevent the Yippee ruckus," she said. But KTVI general manager Ralph Hanson said the axe fell on Peters not because of anything she said but because of lousy ratings. Callers who flooded the KTVI and *Globe-Democrat* switchboards weren't enough to bring Peters back.

For several years, she shut herself off, in part because of the death of her husband, Willie, in 1974. She appeared in local theater productions, but there was no way she could get another local show. Those had ended, since the cost was too high. But in 1977, she and other family members opened a local barbecue place called Charlotte's Rib. In her book *Charlotte!: The First Lady of Saint Louis Television,* Peters's daughter Patricia Peters Schwarz said Peters said a word to her late husband just before the restaurant opened. "Hey Willie! Guess what? I've got my audience back and with a whole new bag of goodies! Isn't that great, Willie? Isn't that great?" She died in 1988 but is still remembered fondly by all who watched her antics on TV. The woman who started as a girl dancing on top of a bar ended with encores at a restaurant.

# Redd Foxx: Junk Man

Most of America knows Redd Foxx as the hyper-grumpy junk dealer in reruns of the sitcom *Sanford and Son*. He was sure to get laughs when he feigned a heart attack or gruffly scolded his son with two words: "You dummy." What they may not know is that Foxx started his life of making people chortle as a kid in St. Louis. Born in 1922, Foxx would lie in bed next to a radio listening to Fred Allen and the comedy series *Myrt and Marge* and dream of making people laugh the same way. Eventually he would. People today know him best as Redd Foxx, but his name was actually Jon (or John, depending on the source) Elroy Sanford.

The upheavals started when Jon was about four, and his father walked out on his family. Suddenly a single mother, Jon's mother moved to Chicago to make more money as a domestic. She left Jon and his brother Fred Jr. with their grandmother, who lived in a shack. Soon after that, their mother sent Jon and his brother to Milwaukee, where they attended an all-black Catholic school. Homesick and causing problems in class, Jon came back to live with his grandmother in 1931. Fred Jr. followed a year later. Jon had a reputation as a class cutup and school goof-off at Banneker Elementary School at Lucas and Ewing. A year after he started at Banneker, Jon was expelled for tossing a book at a teacher. After that, ten-year-old Jon and his fourteen-year-old brother were sent off to Chicago to live with their mother.

At school in Chicago, Jon's reputation for keeping people laughing grew, even as he got a reputation as a troublemaker as a member of the 58th Street Gang. He dropped out of high school at sixteen and tried to make a go as a professional musician. In 1938, he moved to New York, where he played in a three-man washboard band and eventually changed his name to Redd Foxx. He played in the Apollo Theater in Harlem and on the Chitlin' Circuit with the comedian Slappy White in the 1950s. His lines, typical of the working class, weren't for kids. Foxx and White sold more than fifteen million copies of records full of blue humor. "That's the humor I heard in the ghettos. They didn't pull no punches, and they didn't want to hear about Little Boy Blue and Cinderella. So I gave them what they wanted. I busted loose," he said.

Foxx shifted to white audiences, entertaining at places like Caesar's Palace in Las Vegas and telling jokes himself on such shows as *The Today Show* and *The Tonight Show*. His Los Angeles nightclub, Redd's Place, attracted comedians like Bill Cosby, Flip Wilson, and Richard Pryor. Then producer Norman Lear saw him play in the flick *Cotton Comes to Harlem* and snatched Foxx to play a crusty old junk dealer eking out an existence in a new family sitcom, *Sanford and Son*. On the air from 1972 to 1977, the sitcom was an American redo of a British show, *Steptoe and Son*.

In the American spin-off, Foxx and his son, played by Demond Wilson, lived in Watts, the scene of historic race riots several years earlier. Foxx adopted his original last name of Sanford and the first name of Fred, after his late brother. He brought in African American comedians and performers to show off their talent and introduced storylines dealing with current issues in African American communities. Writer Christine Acham contends that the humor in *Sanford and Son* was a way to look at the harsher realities of black Americans. Fred Sanford, Acham claimed, represented

the trickster, an enduring character in African American storytelling going back to stories of slaves who outsmart their owners. Joel Chandler Harris's Uncle Remus stories, in which the smaller Brer Rabbit, representing blacks, outsmarts bigger animals, is a prime example of trickster stories.

After *Sanford and Son,* Foxx starred in a variety hour and a comedy, but neither lasted. After co-starring with Della Reese in *Harlem Nights* in 1989, CBS hired the two for another sitcom, *The Royal Family.* Ready for a comeback, Foxx died of a massive heart attack on the show's set on October 11, 1991. He was sixty-nine. He was buried in Las Vegas, but part of him remained in St. Louis. He was inducted into the St. Louis Walk of Fame in 1992. Today, his name is remembered on a small street north of the Veterans Administration Cochran Hospital just a few blocks from where he lived on Bell Avenue. The city renamed a small part of West Spring Avenue to Redd Foxx Lane in 1974. Foxx returned to St. Louis to participate in the renaming ceremony. The renamed street recalled a difficult part of Foxx's life. But today it brings to mind the laughs he brought to millions.

# Pokey LaFarge: Guitar Pickin' for America

Pokey LaFarge's plan for life didn't include college. For him, it was better to head to the freeway exit after high school, stick out a thumb, and spend the years after that matriculating in the University of Life. It worked for LaFarge. Starting out in his home of Bloomington, Illinois, in 2001, he went gallivanting around the country and made stops in Louisville, Kentucky, and Asheville, North Carolina, before landing in St. Louis in 2008. In his travels, he has gained a big following for his traditional songs in a style he calls American music. He developed a love for the Gateway City, with all its quirks.

The songs of Pokey LaFarge are a tasty stew of rapid-paced country, early jazz, ragtime, and western swing, backed up by a six-member band that plays guitar, harmonica, washboard, upright bass, drums, horns, clarinet, and sax. He has played mandolin, fiddle, and tenor banjo, but he now favors a 1946 Epiphone Spartan guitar that's often in his hands. A Stetson often tops his slicked-back hair, and a tie and suit frequently complete a look that seems more comfortable in the 1920s than the post-millennium. The tone in his deep nasal voice is all smiles, even when the subject is bad times and the high cost of everything.

In the official video for LaFarge's newest album, *Something in the Water,* his fiancé wields a baseball bat as she chases him down Utah Street. Then they sit lovey-dovey, kissy-kissy on a chair in a South Side backyard. "What makes her crazy, I don't know, never seen anything like her before. Must be something in the water," he sings. In "Central Time," on the album *Pokey LaFarge,* he pays homage to the Midwest when he sings, "The Missouri is my right arm, the Ohio is my left/ But I'm livin' on the Mississippi River where I like life the best/I don't mind the West Coast, and I don't mind the East Coast/Oh, baby, but I ain't gonna live on no coast." In those and the rest of his songs, his exuberant Midwestern style reflects his music.

"I've been an entertainer and a performer and a ham ever since I was born," he said. He began his life as Andrew Heissler in 1983. Fourteen years later, his grandfather from St. Clair County, Illinois—a member of the St. Louis Banjo Club—bought him a super-cheap Chinese guitar to play on. "I was a writer," LaFarge said. "Being an artsy type, I think my grandfather must have seen something, so I got my guitar." He traded it for a Sony Walkman cassette player when he was eighteen, while he was hitchhiking, after he'd been on the road for a while. But it didn't matter. By that time, he was playing mandolin on the street in Eugene, Oregon. From there, he moved to Wisconsin, where he did construction in Madison, Milwaukee, and Madeline Island, a Lake Superior isle two and a half miles off Wisconsin's northern shore. LaFarge self-published his first album, *Marmalade,* in 2006. He took off in 2012, after working with Jack White and signing with Third Man Records. He's had seven albums and has been featured in *Rolling Stone* magazine and on the *Late Show with David Letterman.* He has his own NPR Tiny Desk Concert and travels around the country and the world. Views for his official music video approached nine hundred thousand on YouTube in the spring of 2016.

LaFarge's office is on Cherokee Street, as is his home. The backdrops for many of his music videos are from the South Side, and some of his music is about the Midwest. He's played the Casa Loma Ballroom and filled the Pageant on New Year's Eve. "It's real, all the good and the bad," he said of the Gateway City. "There's not many falsities, pretexts here as there are in such hip places as Nashville or Austin or LA." Besides, "St. Louis is so much more beautiful than Nashville is." Looking back at his career, LaFarge said he has been humbled by his success but not surprised. "I just want to make beautiful music, to be the best person I can be to make people happy," he said. "I don't have a choice. It's what I was put on earth to do." And he wants to do it in St. Louis.

# SPORTS GUYS

# Chris Von der Ahe: No *Dummkopf*

The words of St. Louis Browns owner Chris Von der Ahe, delivered in a mangled German accent, were sure to amuse. After his St. Louis Browns won a game with a hit to right field, he put out word that his players henceforth should hit all balls to right field. He boasted he had the biggest baseball diamond in the world. Told that all diamonds had the same dimensions, he said, "Well I got the biggest infield, anyways." Such quotes made Von der Ahe seem not too *schmart*, but he was no *dummkopf*. "Von der Ahe was no classic clown but a man that modern club owners such as Charles Finley and George Steinbrenner have emulated, even if they didn't realize it," wrote St. Louis baseball writer Jim Rygelski.

Von der Ahe started his life in 1851, far from America and baseball in the German farming community of Westphalia. He came to America in his teens, possibly to avoid the draft. Perhaps attracted by the claim of German writer Gottfried Duden that Missouri was a paradise, he made his way to St. Louis around 1867. While he was still a teenager, he opened a delicatessen and saloon at Spring and Sullivan Avenues. In the 1870s, he started a new food market, saloon, and beer garden at Grand and St. Louis Avenues. Over the years, he began to notice that many of his customers had come from just-finished games of a ball team called the Brown Stockings. Von der Ahe didn't know much about baseball, but he did know how to recognize an opportunity. He bought into the team and owned it outright by the end of 1881. After one game, he said to investor Al Spink, "Vot a fine pig crowd. But the game, Al, how vas the game? Vas it a goot game? You know, I know nothing."

The Brown Stockings, also called the Browns, became part of a new league called the American Association and quickly started bringing in cash for Von der Ahe. Helped by first baseman–manager Charlie Comiskey, the team went on to be champion of the American Association from 1885 to 1888. Years later, Comiskey would own the Chicago White Sox and be the namesake for two of its stadiums. But as Von der Ahe's manager, Comiskey sometimes had to ask his boss to leave when he barged into a dressing room after a game to berate a player for making an error. Von der Ahe built a reputation for threatening to fine players and not following through. He also could be generous, as when he paid for a train trip for a group of fans to attend the world championship game against the New York Giants in 1888.

But "Der Boss President," as people called Von der Ahe, also became known for outrageous promotions, like a scantily clad all-girl band, horse racing, a shoot-the-shoot, and a beer garden. For those who were bored with what went on on the field, he brought in a Wild West show with cowboys, cowgirls, and Indians. Von der Ahe won a court fight against Sunday blue laws prohibiting Sunday pro baseball.

The stunts no longer worked after the American Association folded in the 1890s and the Browns moved to the National League. The team stayed at or near the bottom of the league standings throughout that decade. Von der Ahe changed managers six times in a year and faced a player rebellion. All of this loosened Von der Ahe's hold on the team, but what ended it was a fire that destroyed his ball field in 1898. The Mississippi Valley Trust Co. sued when payments on bonds taken out to finance reconstruction weren't made. Von der Ahe lost the suit, and the team was put up for

auction to pay the bills. With Von der Ahe gone, the team was renamed the Perfectos in 1899 and the Cardinals in 1900. In 1902, a new team from the new American League called the St. Louis Browns started playing in St. Louis.

Von der Ahe returned to life as a saloonkeeper but didn't do well. His excesses caught up with him in 1913, when he succumbed to dropsy and cirrhosis of the liver. He lies today with the city's high and mighty in Bellefontaine Cemetery, beneath a statue of Von der Ahe that was engraved with the year of his death before he died. It looks showy and grandiose, just as Von der Ahe's promotions were showy and grandiose. But they also led the way to events at games today that have nothing to do with baseball, like the Cardinals' kiss cam, the cap dance, and Fredbird. They changed going to a ball game from merely watching an athletic contest to a day at the park.

# Sam Muchnick:
# Mr. Wrestling

I n the fifties, no place in St. Louis meant class like the Chase Park Plaza. Bob Hope, Dean Martin, Sammy Davis Jr., and Frank Sinatra broadcast acts from the hotel's Chase Club, while the traveling super-rich rested their heads on the hostelry's pillows. Part of that hotel was an aircraft hangar–sized dance hall called the Khorassan Room, used for highbrow soirees like the annual Veiled Prophet Ball. It was the height of elegance. But the shrieking hordes that started showing up in the Khorassan in 1959 to cheer on bruisers locking each other in scissor holds were anything but elegant. What was this? Nothing less than a series of wrestling matches broadcast on KPLR Channel 11, a new TV station founded by Chase Park Plaza owner Harold Koplar. The organizer of that series, which was called *Wrestling at the Chase,* was a legendary wrestling promoter named Sam Muchnick.

Nobody could predict Muchnick's important role in the sport when he was born in the Ukraine in 1905. His Jewish parents named him Jeshua Muchnick. Little Jeshua had the blood of a performer in him: his mother once danced for Czar Nicholas II. Jeshua's parents brought him to St. Louis in 1911. A name change was necessary, since Jeshua became Jesus in English, and it's hardly right to call a Jewish boy Jesus. So he became Sammy.

Life was tough for Sammy Muchnick, who lived in the city's Kerry Patch neighborhood, surrounded by Germans, Jews, Italians, and Poles. When he wasn't fighting, he was selling papers. Early on, he fell in love with sports and writing about sports. In 1926, he started work as a sportswriter for the old *St. Louis Times,* even though it paid less than another job as a postal clerk. But how could mere money compare to being there when the Redbirds beat Babe Ruth in the 1926 World Series, or taking infield practice at third base in a Cardinals uniform at the Redbirds spring training

base in Bradenton, Florida, in 1929? Certainly it didn't hold
a candle to hanging out with Frankie Frisch, Babe Ruth, Mae
West, and Al Capone. It seemed too good to end, but it did when
the *Times* merged with the *Star* in 1932. A job was waiting for
Muchnick at the new *Star-Times*, but if he took it a friend would
have to lose his. So Muchnick quit. Bad news? Not for this tough
fighter from Kerry Patch.

Muchnick turned to wrestling and soon was making his daily
bread with Tom Packs, one of the biggest promoters of wrestling
shows in the country. Muchnick had his first wrestling card in
1942 and started a series of shows at the old Arena in 1945.
They would go on for thirty-seven years. He formed the National
Wrestling Alliance with several promoters around the country in
1948, the same year he was asked to do a favor for an old friend,
President Harry Truman. Truman wanted to give a campaign
speech at Kiel the same night as Muchnick's planned wrestling
card. A Democratic Party official asked Muchnick if he could move
his event to another night. "Well, I've got a show," Muchnick said,
"but for the president, I'll change it."

Muchnick and wrestling grew in popularity in the 1950s, but
many would have nothing to do with it. A chance meeting between
Koplar and Muchnick on an airplane helped win over many of the
naysayers. They talked about how great it would be to originate
a local TV wrestling show in the Khorassan, scrawled details on
a napkin, and pronounced the deal done with a handshake. To
announce the show, they signed up Hill neighborhood native Joe
Garagiola, a former Cardinals catcher and color commentator for
then-Cardinals broadcaster Harry Caray. Garagiola wasn't satisfied
to say that Johnny Valentine won a match by smashing his elbow
against the head of an opponent. Garagiola dubbed it "an Arm and
Hammer Baking Soda elbow," and added, "Boy, Valentine must
be a tough guy." At tables nearby, men in black ties and women in
evening gowns ate their filet mignon and cheered the gladiators just
a few feet away.

The show was on the air from 1959 to 1983, but it actually only originated from the Khorassan Room from 1959 until 1967 and again for three months in 1972. No matter. The list of wrestling stars that brawled on the show is long and distinguished: future Minnesota governor Jesse Ventura, Dick Murdoch, "Macho Man" Randy Savage, "Bulldog" Bob Brown, "Wild Bill" Logsdon. In that whole time, Muchnick played an important part both in *Wrestling at the Chase* and in the sport throughout the country. The adulation continued until his retirement in 1982 and his death in 1995. Even today, those who knew him all say that Sam Muchnick was Mr. Wrestling.

# Dizzy Dean:
# Dizzy with Delight

I t was a case of brotherly one-upmanship. Cardinals pitcher Jay Hanna Dean lost a no-hitter in the eighth inning of the first game of a doubleheader against the Brooklyn Dodgers. But he held on for a 1–0 shutout win. When his brother Paul Dean pitched a no-hitter in the second game, Jay quipped, "If'n I'd knowed Paul was gonna throw a no-hitter, well, I'd a throwed one, too." The remark was in perfect form for Jay Dean, who was better known as Dizzy Dean. As one of four National League pitchers to win thirty games in a season under modern regulations, and a four-time league leader in strikeouts, Dean easily won entry to the Baseball Hall of Fame. But it was his quips and antics that made him memorable.

Dean variously told reporters that he was born in a sharecropper's cabin near Lucas, Arkansas, on January 16, 1911; at Holdenville, Oklahoma, on February 22, 1911; and in Bond, Mississippi, on August 22, 1911. Quizzed about the difference, Dizzy said he wanted to give each newshound who asked him an original story. The correct story was the one that said Dean was born near Lucas, Arkansas. Dizzy and his brother Paul had a natural inclination toward pitching. In 1930, Dizzy started pitching for the Houston Buffalos. When the White Sox played an

exhibition game against the Buffaloes, White Sox coach Bernard (Mike) Kelly said, "That kid is making you look dizzy." The nickname stuck.

Dean awed opponents and fans from the first day of his first full season with the Cardinals, 1932. He won eighteen and lost fifteen that year and posted a 20–18 win-loss record in 1933. While other teams were learning the bad news about his pitching, fans were learning about his antics. In one instance, the whole team went looking for Dean's lucky sock. They stopped when someone noticed it was on Dizzy's foot.

It was preparation for 1934, the high point of Dean's career. Paul joined Dizzy as a pitcher and won nineteen games. Combined with Dizzy's thirty wins, the two were responsible for forty-nine of the Cardinals' ninety-five victories that year. Dizzy announced a third brother was pitching in Houston. It turned out that his brother Elmer Dean was pitching peanuts as a vendor at the Houston ballpark. Reporters called the 1934 Cardinals the Gashouse Gang because of the rough way members looked and played. Facing the Detroit Tigers in that year's World Series, the Dean brothers earned all four Redbird wins, just as Dizzy boasted would happen. In a long explanation to *Post-Dispatch* reporter J. Roy Stockton, Dizzy said he was just telling his bosses what they could expect from them in the series. From then on, the explanation became, "It ain't braggin' if you can do it."

Prospects were bright for Dizzy, but they darkened after he started the 1937 All-Star Game for the National League. Earl Averill's line drive back to the mound broke Dizzy's big toe. That was bad enough, but the killer came when Dean came back too soon. He dealt with the broken toe by changing the way he pitched. That injured his arm and took away his edge. The Cubs bought him the next year, but he only won seven games in the regular season. He didn't have his stuff in a 6–3 loss to the Yankees in the second game of the 1938 World Series, but neither did anybody else. The Yanks won four games straight. Dizzy somehow made it into 1941 for the Cubs but only as a has-been.

Dean was finished as a ballplayer, but he still had his mouth and put it to good use as a broadcaster. Starting in 1941, he did double duty as a broadcaster on station KWK for the Cardinals and the St. Louis Browns. English teachers hated how he butchered the language. He said "slud" instead of "slid" and was heard saying, "Now there's George Kurowski at the plate, and he's a-gonna bunt." But he had the fans listening to KWK and drinking the Falstaff beer he hawked. Complaining about Browns pitchers in 1947, he said, "I could beat nine out of ten who call themselves" pitchers today. He suited up and blanked the White Sox for four innings. He went on to tell stories as a baseball broadcaster on national TV. Then he and his wife retired to Bond, Mississippi. He invested in oil and Texas real estate and became a millionaire before he died in 1974. In his shortened career, he won 150 games and lost 83. But those in the stands will always know him as the Redbirds' all-time prankster and language-mangler.

# Bob Broeg: The Happy Sports Scribbler

When he talked to a big league ballplayer or banged out another column, Bob Broeg was like a kid on the playground. He was the scribbler with the inside track on St. Louis sports for more than a half a century. Never satisfied with plain vanilla wording, this master of phrasing always found a new way to jazz up his yarns. For example, in a 1983 column relinquishing his title as lead sports columnist for the *Post-Dispatch* to Kevin Horrigan, Broeg described his successor as "the olive-skinned fleshy wit" and as "healthy as the next club sandwich." And how did he pronounce his name? "Broeg as in plague."

With that ever-present bow tie, Bob Broeg hung out with the rich and the famous, but he began his life in a simpler fashion, in the kitchen of the family home at Virginia Avenue and Pulaski Street on the South Side. The doctor who delivered him scarred his left eye with a forceps, causing permanent blurring. The forceps' other tong went into the back of his cranium. "So, yeah, I had a hole in my head from day one," he declared.

Early on, the family encouraged young Bob's interest in writing and sports. A favorite memory was standing next to the visitors' dugout at Sportsman's Park and getting Babe Ruth's autograph. So began a lifetime love of athletic competition. That love blossomed through four years at his beloved University of Missouri at Columbia, years covering sports for the Associated Press in Boston and the *St. Louis Star-Times*, and a stint in the marines. It was fabulous, but for him life didn't really start until he started writing for the *Post-Dispatch* in 1945.

Broeg soon got a reputation for getting scoops and even making news. Covering a Cardinals-Dodgers game in Brooklyn, Broeg got curious about a noise heard whenever Stan Musial came up to bat. He discovered that the weary Brooklyn fans were bemoaning another home plate visit of "the Man." Broeg wrote about it, and from then on people called him Stan the Man. Broeg got another scoop in 1951, when St. Louis Browns owner Bill Veeck gave him a tip over some beers. The next day, Veeck told Broeg, he would bring a three-foot-seven-inch dwarf named Eddie Gaedel up to bat. Broeg brought in a photographer who ventured onto the field and knelt near the dwarf. The picture and the dwarf made history, and Broeg was there.

Broeg moved up to sports editor in 1958. He was generally easygoing but was known to get riled. Cardinals broadcaster Jack Buck spoke of how Broeg didn't get along with Harry Caray, who was fired as Cardinals broadcaster in 1969 and became the voice of the Cubs. "It's a wonder Broeg never punched Harry, because Broeg has a temper, and he lets you know where he stands," Buck said. But he did deck a drunk with a single punch while he was covering the 1960 Pirates-Yankees World Series. The offense? The man looked into Broeg's bag filled with milk and cookies and knocked it from his hands.

There were times, St. Louis sports journalist Greg Marecek recalls, when Broeg got so peeved that he tossed a typewriter across the *Post-Dispatch* newsroom. But Marecek knows the other side of Broeg as well. Broeg could have ignored Marecek when he encountered him at an event in 1972. Marecek went on to be a broadcaster, author, and founder of the St. Louis Sports Hall of Fame. But back then, he was in his first year as sports editor of the *South Side Journal.* "I became kind of like the son he never had," Marecek said. Broeg stayed close to Marecek while he worked and after he retired in 1985. Later, as president of the sports radio station KFNS, Marecek called on Broeg to write two hundred five-minute radio spots that were read on the air by Bob Costas in 1999. Those became the basis of the last of Broeg's twenty books, *The 100 Greatest Moments in St. Louis Sports.* One of the editors of that book was Josh Stevens, who now is publisher of Reedy Press. Stevens recalled Broeg's kindness to everyone he met, big and small. On stops at the Schnucks Market at Clayton Road and Lindbergh Boulevard to buy carrot juice and shortbread cookies, he loved exchanging sports banter with a bagger who also was a ticket taker at Busch Stadium. The book came out in 2000, five years before his death, and brought a long list of accolades like this one by *Post-Dispatch* lead sports columnist Bernie Miklasz: "He knew he wanted to be a sportswriter. He'd done it—run off to join the circus—and was more than happy to encourage other dreamers to do the same."

# Gussie Busch: Crown Prince of the Redbirds

Most people who remember Gussie Busch picture him as the St. Louis Cardinals owner who joyfully ran the team for more than forty-five years and made it a source of pride for St. Louis. Oddly, though, Busch preferred other sports early on. He favored riding horses, shooting, boxing, rodeo riding, and the rough and tumble of running the nation's leading brewery. August Anheuser "Gussie" Busch Jr. was born in the last year of the 1800s to a family that was both German aristocracy and Gilded Age big business barons.

He spent much of his childhood living at a massive French Renaissance chateau and hunting lodge on the property where Ulysses Grant once farmed before he became president. Gussie's childhood was one of privilege. He made several trips with his grandfather Adolphus to Germany before the elder Busch died. But he didn't learn much at school. He never graduated from high

school. Gussie started working with the family business soon after Prohibition prevented the family from selling its primary product.

When the ban ended in April 1933, Gussie arranged for a team of Clydesdales to bring a wagon carrying the first case of Budweiser to President Franklin D. Roosevelt at the White House. From that came the Clydesdales seen in so many commercials. The suicide of Gussie's father in 1934 while suffering from a painful bout with dropsy, gout, and heart disease brought his older brother Adolphus to control of the brewery. Power passed to Gussie when Adolphus died in 1946.

Gussie worked to reverse Anheuser-Busch's drop in beer sales from first place in the nation. "Being second means slop," he said. An opportunity arose in 1953 to improve the company's fortunes when St. Louis Cardinals owner Fred Saigh faced fifteen months in prison and had to sell the team. Gussie persuaded Anheuser-Busch to buy the Cardinals. "I'm going at this from the sports angle and not as a sales weapon for Budweiser beer," he said. But it was just part of an effort to turn up the beer spigots. It worked. The company soon was the nation's leading brewer. It still holds that position.

The year after the brewery acquired the Redbirds, the Busches opened Grant's Farm in 1954 for tours. Gussie joined with St. Louis Zoo director George P. Vierheller in welcoming a bottle-fed baby elephant to Grant's Farm for visitors to enjoy. Schoolchildren feasted their eyes on camels from Arabia, a herd of bison, and English stags. Meanwhile, Busch went through a succession of unsuccessful managers in his effort to bring a world championship to St. Louis. But starting in 1964, the team won six National League pennants with Gussie as its president. It opened the new Busch Memorial Stadium downtown in 1966. The Redbirds also won World Series championships in 1964, 1967, and 1982.

Watching the Cardinals play relaxed Gussie but so did gin rummy. Late Missouri senator Thomas Eagleton recalled that Busch sometimes played for hours as a way to relax himself from the tension of the day. He was always adding rules in his favor and reveled in the loud arguments in the competitions. Gin rummy may have taken Gussie's mind off work, but it didn't keep his son August Busch III from seizing control of Anheuser-Busch from him in 1975. Gussie was left with one thing after the palace coup: control of the Cardinals. Redbirds fans became used to the sight of Gussie Busch riding a wagon led by Clydesdales around Busch Stadium. With the help of Al Fleishman, the brewery's public relations genius, Gussie was deeply loved in St. Louis. But even Fleishman couldn't hide all of Gussie's messes. A noted womanizer, he saw his second and third marriages end in ugly divorces, while he outlived his first and fourth wives. A variety of embarrassing and underreported incidents involved Gussie's kids.

It didn't matter. When Gussie died at age ninety, two days before the end of the 1989 season, the city mourned. Cardinals broadcaster Mike Shannon offered a memory of a beer baron with a common touch. "You know, there weren't too many things that Gussie liked to do better than to duck into a corner bar, a little neighborhood tavern, and drink draft beer with people he didn't even know. He just liked to hear what they were talking about." He was king. He loved his subjects, and they loved him.

# Bill Veeck: When Bill Veeck Came to Town

With all the stunts he pulled, Bill Veeck was better suited to own a circus. He wound up filling more seats for baseball teams he owned in Milwaukee, Cleveland, Chicago, and St. Louis with tacky gimmicks like scoreboards that exploded after home runs, live lobster giveaways, and hiring a clown as a coach. The Hall of Fame baseball team owner is best known for bringing in a dwarf for one at bat for his St. Louis Browns. But in St. Louis, he might have been known for something much bigger, had he succeeded in his campaign to make the Browns the city's only ball team.

The son of a president of the Chicago Cubs, Veeck acquired the minor league Milwaukee Brewers in 1941, at the age of twenty-seven. He pumped up attendance by serving free cornflake breakfasts at morning games started for overnight workers at World War II defense plants and by bringing the previously losing Brewers three American Association pennants in a row. In 1946, he bought the Cleveland Indians, and the following year he signed Larry Doby as the first black player in the American League. Legendary pitcher Satchel Paige came to the team in 1948, the same year the Indians won a world championship. But Veeck needed money to settle his divorce from his first wife and sold the Indians in 1949. In July 1951, he bought the struggling St. Louis Browns in mid-season and immediately shook things up.

In 1951, the Browns would end the year forty-six games out of first place. Its best regular hitter averaged

Bill Veeck signs Satchel Paige to a St. Louis Browns contract.

.261, and only one pitcher won more than six games. But Veeck thought big. He celebrated his acquisition with a fireworks display between the two games of a twi-night doubleheader and gave out free bottles of beer and soda to everybody who showed up.

It seemed that Veeck's main job was to resell the Browns to St. Louis. But in his autobiography, he claimed that his plan was to drive the Redbirds out of St. Louis. He would do it by getting under the skin of Cardinals owner Fred Saigh. As owner of Sportsman's Park, where both teams played, he decorated the whole stadium with Browns memorabilia. He filled the lineup with former Cardinals and a pitcher who never played for the Cardinals—Satchel Paige. He named Cardinals greats Dizzy Dean as an announcer and Rogers Hornsby and Marty Marion as managers.

But Veeck's biggest strike for the hearts of St. Louis was the one that certified him forever as baseball's greatest showman. Six weeks after he bought the Browns, he brought out number 1/8, a three-foot-seven-inch, sixty-five-pound dwarf named Eddie Gaedel to bat at the start of the second game of a doubleheader with the Detroit Tigers. When plate umpire Eddie Hurley objected, Browns manager Zack Taylor produced a contract. Photographers scrambled to get a picture of Gaedel holding a toy bat. Hurley wouldn't allow catcher Bob Swift to lie down to give pitcher Bobby

Cain a better target. Nor would he allow Cain to pitch underhand. Cain hurled four balls over Gaedel's head. Gaedel trotted to first base and into the history books. The establishment huffed, but the nation and St. Louis loved it. With stunts like that, attendance skyrocketed from 293,790 in 1951 to 518,796 in 1952. Cardinals attendance plummeted by a similar amount.

But then came news that Saigh faced fifteen months in prison for tax evasion and was looking for a buyer for the Cardinals. Offers came from Houston and Milwaukee. When Anheuser-Busch announced in February 1953 that it would buy the Cardinals and keep them in St. Louis, Veeck knew everything was over. He couldn't compete with the beer barons. He talked to people in Milwaukee and Los Angeles before selling the team to Baltimore businessmen, who moved the team to their city in 1954 and renamed it the Orioles.

Veeck left St. Louis and never gave the city another thought. In 1959, he led a group that bought a controlling interest in the Chicago White Sox. Under Veeck, the White Sox won the American League pennant for the first time in forty years and set attendance records. He retired for health reasons in 1961 but returned as owner in 1975. Attendance again soared. At Disco Demolition Night, disco records brought in by fans were blown up between games of a doubleheader with the Detroit Tigers. Fans flooded the field, and the second game was forfeited to the Tigers. Such shenanigans may have built Veeck's reputation, but it was free agency that forced him to sell the team in 1981. He never lost interest in the game, though. Ten days before he died of cancer in 1986, Veeck asked a friend if he thought he could buy the Cleveland Indians.

# Yogi Berra: The Phenom of Elizabeth Avenue

After the Arch and Ted Drewes, every St. Louisan should take out-of-town relatives or friends to the 5400 block of Elizabeth Avenue on the Hill. Especially if that relative or friend is so deluded as to root for the Yankees. For in front of one of the block's immaculate homes with cut-by-scissors lawns is a marker set in the sidewalk announcing that Yogi Berra grew up in the house in front of the viewer. Across that street is another marker proclaiming that the major league catcher and Hall of Fame broadcaster Joe Garagiola grew up in the house in front of it. On this street, Yogi first learned the game he would love and play the rest of his life. A visit to the block offers a reminder that Yogi was as much a product of St. Louis as toasted ravioli.

Yogi was born on the Hill on May 12, 1925, to Pietro and Pauline Berra, immigrants from Malvaglio, Italy. He was one of five Berra children in the Italian working-class neighborhood. A friend gave him the name Yogi because he decided Berra looked like a practitioner of yoga—a "yogi"—when he sat down. He was always getting his friends to play a game, be it baseball, football, or whatever was popular at the moment. For softball games played on Elizabeth Avenue, Yogi had bases and base lines painted on the blacktop. It wrecked his dad's best brushes, but you gotta do what you gotta do. "Growing up in St. Louis, we used to play pickup games in Sublette Park and the empty lot down near my house on Elizabeth Avenue, and we played because we loved it," he wrote in his book *You Can Observe a Lot by Watching: What I've Learned about Teamwork from the Yankees and Life*. It's one of several volumes Yogi wrote that depended on his convoluted way of talking to make sales.

Yogi loved baseball, but he hated school. That led to a significant moment Yogi described in another book that takes its title from one of his mangled attempts to communicate. *When You Come to a Fork in the Road, Take It!* describes a meeting at the end of the eighth grade over his desire to quit school to go to work. "My parents, the principal, and the parish priest all had a conference and tried to talk me into continuing, but I was a lousy student and pretty stubborn and felt I was wasting my time. I remember a teacher once asking me, 'Don't you know anything?' and I said 'I don't even suspect anything.'" They let him quit and take that fork in the road, as long as he handed over to his mother all his earnings from working in a shoe factory.

Yogi took another critical fork in the road in 1942 because of a misjudgment by the great and usually infallible Cardinals general manager Branch Rickey. The story goes that Rickey offered both Garagiola and Yogi contracts to sign with the Cardinals. Garagiola was offered a $500 signing bonus; Berra wasn't. When Berra stalled, Rickey offered a $250 bonus and told Yogi he probably wouldn't make it to the majors. "I want the same as Joey's getting," Yogi said. The negotiations ended, and Berra later signed with the Yankees. Longtime *Post-Dispatch* sports editor Bob Broeg grieved that the loss of Yogi Berra was one reason why the Yankees did so much better than the Cardinals in the two decades that followed.

As a Yankee, Yogi was an All-Star fifteen times and an American League Most Valuable Player three times. He helped his team win ten world championships. "Yogi had the fastest bat I ever saw," said teammate Hector Lopez. Yankees manager Casey Stengel said his club's pitching was so good because of Yogi's prowess as a catcher. Said Stengel: "He looks cumbersome but he's quick as a cat." Named to the Hall of Fame in 1972, Yogi was part of seven pennant winners and three world champion teams as a coach and manager. Regardless of what team they favored, baseball fans everywhere mourned Yogi's death in 2015 at the age of ninety. Others who couldn't tell a foul ball from a fly ball chuckled at his passing when they thought of their favorite "Yogi-isms"—sentences like "A nickel ain't worth a dime anymore," "It gets late early out here," and "If the world were perfect, it wouldn't be" seem to make no sense whatsoever. But to those who think about them, they make perfect sense and contain real wisdom. Wisdom from the Hill.

# Bob Uecker: Bob Uecker Blows His Horn

Bob Uecker bombed in six years as a major leaguer, but he cashed in afterward by joking about it. As a broadcaster for the Milwaukee Brewers, as a movie star, as a comedian, and as a regular on late-night talk shows, he showed the kind of comedic timing he lacked as a .200 lifetime hitter. "For any player who's ever played with a championship team, the awarding of the rings is the culmination of the whole season," he said on the *Late Show with David Letterman* in 1994. He spoke, of course, of being a backup catcher for the Cardinals when the team won the World Series in 1964. "I can remember the following year standing there when they threw mine in the outfield." Despite Uecker's struggles on the field, he had one thing going for him: he was the team's championship tuba player in the '64 Series.

The '64 Cardinals World Series victory came eight years after the Milwaukee native signed with the Milwaukee Braves in 1956. He spent six years in the minors before being called up as a backup catcher. He saw limited action in the 1962 season and played in the minor leagues for the Braves in 1963. The next year, the Braves traded him to the Cardinals, who played him as backup to Cardinals catcher Tim McCarver, later a nationally known TV baseball announcer. People generally said Uecker was a good defensive player, which was a nice way of saying he couldn't hit. Strangely, he had some hitting success against Hall of Fame Los Angeles Dodgers pitcher Sandy Koufax. Uecker hit Koufax so well that Koufax once walked him intentionally to get to the pitcher.

In the summer of 1964, Uecker's on-field performance attracted the interest of two students at Drury College (now Drury University) in Springfield, Missouri. Brothers Mark and Paul Stillwell studied the stats and realized that the Cardinals were winless in every game in which Uecker played that year until July 2.

Mark wasn't just any student. He was sports editor of the *Drury Mirror* and years later returned to the college as its director of sports information. They formed a fan club that quickly attracted more than five hundred members. It cranked out sweatshirts with his name and picture and a matchbook with the words "Bob Uecker Is a Great American."

Uecker ignored the fan club until somebody mailed him a scrapbook with clippings detailing how badly he was doing. "Turning the pages, my entire career passes before my eyes. It was a little like drowning," Uecker wrote in his book *Catcher in the Wry*. Despite Uecker's struggles in '64, he would have his moment in the sun. On the last day of August, Uecker drove in the winning run of a game against the Braves. With that 5–4 victory, the Cardinals pulled within two games of the second-place Reds. The Cardinals kept winning, while the league-leading Phillies collapsed. The Redbirds won the National League pennant on the last game of the season and faced the Yankees in the World Series.

Uecker might have been a lucky charm for the Cardinals, but manager Johnny Keane stayed with his starting catcher. McCarver batted .478, stole a base, and was a key to the Cardinals seven-game victory against the Yankees. But Uecker didn't just sit on the bench. Before the beginning of one home game early in the series, he noticed a lonely tuba lying in the left field corner. A player for a Dixieland band had left it behind while he took a break with the rest of the band. Sensing an opportunity, Uecker picked it up and started catching balls in it. A picture taken of him at the time shows him apparently playing the instrument.

Young Greg Marecek was in the bleachers when Bob Uecker made this memorable play. "He came out of the dugout, and he had the tuba," said Marecek, who went on to be a sportswriter and the founder and president of the St. Louis Sports Hall of Fame. "He just started blowing it." Uecker bowed, and people cheered. Eventually, the Cardinals got a bill for the repair of a dented rim. Uecker happily paid part of the bill.

The next season, Uecker improved his record to a career-best .228. But that didn't impress the Cardinals brass. The president of Uecker's fan club sent the team management an angry letter when he was traded to the Phillies at the end of the season. In 1967, he was traded back to the Braves after they moved to Atlanta, and he ended his career that year. "Anybody with ability can play in the big leagues," he would write in *Catcher in the Wry*. "To last as long as I did with the skills I had, with the numbers I produced, was a triumph of the human spirit."

# Mickey Garagiola: The Important Garagiola Brother

People who didn't know much only knew Mickey Garagiola as Joe Garagiola's big brother. But around St. Louis, Mickey was well known in his own right. He was known as St. Louis's most famous waiter, and he claimed he was present during the accidental invention of toasted ravioli. He was an announcer for the iconic sports program *Wrestling at the Chase.* Fact is, many in St. Louis who wanted a standout night of eating out might say, "Forget Joe, get me Mickey."

Mickey grew up on the Hill in the twenties and thirties in an atmosphere that was half America and half Italy. His parents

were born near Milan, Italy, and raised their kids in the 5400 block of Elizabeth. In that block, Joe Garagiola and Yogi Berra, a neighbor, organized the games that prepared them for life in big league baseball. Mickey recalled that his father waited outside the house for a ride to his job at a brickyard two miles away. When he returned at 4:30 p.m., Mickey and Joe were ready with a bucket of beer. After Mickey graduated from eighth grade at St. Ambrose grade school, his dad got him a part-time job at a Hill restaurant named Ruggeri's.

Mickey started as a dishwasher in 1936 and stayed there for forty-six years.

Mickey moved from washing dishes to waiting tables, a job he felt was made for him, especially the part about the tips. "Going home with fifteen or twenty dollars in your pocket, man, that was great," Mickey said. "I thought I was rich." Restaurant meals in the Hill restaurants were stunning, no matter where you ate. Mickey contended he witnessed St. Louis culinary history one night after his shift ended at Ruggeri's. Not feeling sleepy, he wandered over to Oldani's Tavern, now Mama Campisi's. There, he claimed, he was present when a worker at Oldani's supposedly dropped an order of ravioli into boiling oil rather than boiling water. Rather than waste it, the bar's owner served it to customers with red sauce. That was the birth of toasted ravioli, Mickey insisted. Owners of restaurants like Charlie Gitto's also make the same claims. The truth is that nobody knows. But Mickey stood by his claim.

Mickey could tell the story to Ruggeri's customers like Rosemary Clooney, Mae West, and Frank Sinatra. Be they politicians, big league ballplayers, or top-notch entertainers, they made it to Ruggeri's. A favorite customer was Detroit Tigers manager Mayo Smith. As the Tigers were celebrating their World Series victory over the Cardinals in 1968, Smith ripped off the top of his champagne-soaked jersey and handed it to Joe Garagiola, who was standing nearby. "Give this to Mickey for all the beautiful nights we spent together," Smith said.

Mickey had bunches of such customers by the end of the 1960s who were ready to wrestle anybody who said somebody else was the best waiter in St. Louis. It wasn't surprising, then, that wrestling promoter Sam Muchnick asked him to visit a taping of Channel 11's *Wrestling at the Chase*. Muchnick asked Mickey to read the names and weights from three-by-five cards and then said, "You're my ring announcer."

Mickey settled in to the job, but things didn't always go well. He got a reputation for running from the announcer's table when a bruiser of a wrestler came toward him. Viewers once heard Mickey saying, "Don't hurt me," when Dick "the Bruiser" approached Mickey in a threatening manner. And then there was a certain boo-boo that occurred at the end of a tag-team match pitting Ted DiBiase and Paul Orndorff against world champion Harley Race and Bulldog Bob Brown. When DiBiase pinned Race, Mickey proclaimed, "The *new* world champion . . . Ted DiBiase." But Race couldn't lose the world championship in a tag-team match. Larry Matysik, the main announcer, explained that. Mickey was distraught, and Muchnick had to calm him down.

The program brought local fame to Mickey among those who never came to the Hill, but it was just a small part of his week. Most of it was spent at Ruggeri's burnishing his reputation as a top-flight waiter. That ended one Saturday night in 1982, when a member of the Ruggeri family told employees the restaurant was closing. Then Mickey asked the owners of another Hill restaurant, Pietro's, if they had an opening. They did, and Mickey kept working until his seventy-sixth birthday in 1996. From then until he died in 2010, Mickey reminisced with friends and talked with his brother Joe on the phone. More people may have seen Joe on TV, but for restaurant customers Mickey served at Ruggeri's and Pietro's, and for those who saw him on *Wrestling at the Chase,* he was Joe Garagiola's big brother in more ways than age.

# Zip Rzeppa:
# Life after the Zippos

Zip Rzeppa's Zippo Awards segment was a two-hundred-mile-an-hour combination of demolition derby and extreme skiing with a voice-over faster than an auctioneer. With Billy Joel's supersonic "Root Beer Rag" banging in the background, viewers of Rzeppa's Friday night sports shows might see frenzied clips of impossible catches, goofy pitches over the catcher's head, and the best camel wrestling of the week. "It was all fast paced, and I would play off the reaction of the anchors," Rzeppa said of the nearly three-minute segment, which was actually the Zippo Awards for the Best, the Worst, and the Weirdest Performances in the Wild and Wacky Wonderful World of Sports. It was a major reason why Rzeppa made $350,000 a year as KMOV-TV sports director.

But he walked away from the job. Two decades later, he's convinced he did the right thing, because he did it for a greater purpose.

Christopher Rzeppa got the nickname Zip because of the way he zipped passes as quarterback for his high school football team in Detroit. After graduating from Boston University in 1974, he zipped his way through TV sports reporting jobs to a position in Boston. He'd been developing the Zippo Awards since early in his career. The segment was fully formed when he took a sports director job at KTVI Channel 2 in 1984. In 1988, he became sports director of KMOV.

It seemed everything was going right for Rzeppa in 1995. But it wasn't. After working for nineteen years at six television stations in five cities, he was burned out. "I loved the job, but I knew there was more to life than working all the time." So he quit. He kept doing the Zippos but was otherwise without income. His solution was to start a nationally syndicated Saturday morning radio program called the *Great American Sports Trivia Show!* It ran in fifty-seven markets, but needed to be in two hundred markets for national advertisers to support it. The program flopped. Doors were closing, but one flew open for Rzeppa, who is a faithful Catholic. "God put me on a spiritual path I never asked for. I never envisioned it," he said.

As part of it, Rzeppa knocked on doors in inner-city parishes asking people if they wanted to learn more about the Catholic faith. Some thought he was a detective. Others asked, "Did you come to put me on the Zippo Awards?" An elderly woman once told Rzeppa and his partner, Declan Duffy, "I wouldn't hang around here, there was a shooting here last night." Thankfully, Rzeppa said, nobody was harmed in this four-year project, and there actually were a few conversions. "We trusted in the protection of the Blessed Mother," Rzeppa said.

During this period, in 1996, he got a full-time job helping people with mental or physical disabilities at MERS (Metropolitan Employment and Rehabilitation Services), now MERS Goodwill. He started at a mere $22,500. "I wasn't working for $22,500 because I couldn't find a better paying job. I was working there because I wanted to serve," he said. He earned additional money by making new Zippo Awards segments and doing brief segments for WIL radio. New management at KMOV killed the Zippos in 2001, but not before he got a mention of Pope John Paul II into the segment when the pontiff came to St. Louis in 1999. He replaced the face of St. Louis Blues goal scorers with the pope's face. "The puck is sent out in front, and the pope scores!!!!!"

Rzeppa worked his way up to vice president of community affairs at MERS Goodwill. He used his talents as executive director of the St. Louis Council of St. Vincent de Paul from 2006 to 2011 and then spent about a year as managing director of Angels' Arms, a foster care organization. In 2012, he resigned to found Mater Media, a publishing company focusing on evangelizing the Catholic faith. By the end of 2015, the company had produced two books he wrote, the autobiographical *For a Greater Purpose: My Life Journey* and his novel, *My Rock and Salvation.* He plans to expand to publish books by other authors with a Catholic message.

For his company, Rzeppa regularly gives talks to audiences of anywhere from 30 to 210 at churches—mostly Catholic—about his faith. Over the years, he's been a popular Catholic local speaker and fundraiser, even a Catholic evangelist. "Another way to put it is, I'm a witness to the Catholic faith," he said. Rzeppa may not get as much worldly glory out of it as he did at Channel 4, but he doesn't mind. He's got more important things to do than show clips of wrestling camels.

# Ernie Hays: The Music Man of Busch Stadium

When a manager decided it was time to stroll out to the mound for a conversation with a pitcher, Ernie Hays knew just what to do. He'd lay his fingers on the keys, and fifty thousand fans would hear the sound of the "Mickey Mouse March" played on a gargantuan organ. For forty years, in two stadiums and through eight managers, five pennants, and two world championships, Hays and his organ provided the musical voice of the Cardinals. When the game was on, he'd be as focused as any sportswriter, absorbing the details of every play, so he could respond with just the right ditty. But between innings, he was at ease, ready with a joke, especially the unrepeatable kind.

"You would walk into the organist's booth during the game. He'd make you laugh," said baseball writer Greg Marecek. He saw Hays at work from the time he first played for the Cardinals in 1971 to his retirement in 2010 and his death in 2012 at the age of seventy-seven. In 2016, Hays was initiated into the St. Louis Sports Hall of Fame. Cardinals fans knew well his rendition of "Here Comes the King," the thinly veiled Budweiser commercial belted out during a late-inning break. "He was kind of a high-strung guy. He was always motivated," Marecek said.

His repertoire was versatile. Urged by friends, he played the theme from a popular adult movie of the 1970s. It was well known in some circles but apparently not among the Cardinals brass. Nobody stopped him. After third baseman Scott Rolen smacked his thirty-first homer of the 2002 season, Busch Stadium filled with smoke from celebratory fireworks. Hays responded with "Smoke Gets in Your Eyes." Sometimes, he played a tune called "Maria Denise," written by first baseman Pedro Guerrero in honor of his wife, Denise. It was a variation of his practice of playing different songs for each player when he was introduced. He got permission from players to perform the songs they preferred. For Ozzie Smith, for example, he played the theme from *The Wizard of Oz.* He loved to play "St. Louis Blues," the "William Tell Overture," and, of course, "Take Me Out to the Ball Game." In the 1980s, besides lessons, weddings, and funerals that kept him busy enough, he played at such events as an All-American Extravaganza over Independence Day, an organ concert at Laumeier Park amphitheater, and an old-fashioned sing-along marking the opening of the nineteenth season of the Repertory Theatre of St. Louis.

For those who knew this son of St. Louis, it was clear he was headed for a career in music from the moment he was born on New Year's Day in 1935. His mom, a seamstress, sang in her church choir and played the guitar. His dad, who worked for the Chevy division of General Motors, played the banjo. He started piano lessons at eight and performed at dance parties in college. After marrying Loreta

Heriford in 1954, he worked as a disc jockey and news announcer. He spent time in the navy, got a degree in electrical engineering, and worked at the old McDonnell Aircraft and Western Electric. In 1971, he tried out for an opening as an organist for the Cardinals and got the job. That would have been enough to keep anyone busy. But he also held on to his day job working as an engineering supervisor for the old Bell System until 1977. He became a full-time musician and teacher and once played for seven teams at the same time, including the football Cardinals, the Blues, the Steamers and Stars soccer teams, the Spirits of St. Louis basketball team, and St. Louis University. He once remarked that he was never at home when he still worked as an engineer.

Hays's daughter, Pamela Hays Hagstrom, recalls that on Friday nights she would spend time watching her father play at soccer games, and on Saturday nights she would be with him at hockey games. Showing his variety, Hays once asked his daughter if she wanted to go with him to a concert of the rock musician Alice Cooper. "He said that Alice would put on an interesting show, and he was curious." Away from the keyboard, he was a private pilot, had a helicopter license later in life, and was also a certified hypnotherapist. He hypnotized his daughter to ease the pain of childbirth and to help her sleep. "I told him not to ask me any incriminating questions when he put me under," she said. But what almost everyone knows him best for is for the way his fingers made the organ sound at any kind of sports event in St. Louis.

# REBELS WITH A CAUSE

# Josephine Baker: No Friend of St. Louis

Josephine Baker started her life foraging for food in a St. Louis ghetto full of disease. The racism of the surrounding white community bore down upon her. But she did have one advantage: the ragtime music around her after she was born in 1906 was some of the richest anywhere. Her knowledge of that music enabled her to escape the racism and poverty in St. Louis and find a new life in Paris. There she would achieve lasting fame as a singer and exotic dancer, a member of the French Resistance during World War II, and a fighter for civil rights. She always held the racism of the town of her birth in disdain.

Josephine Baker's mother was Carrie McDonald, a washerwoman and vaudeville performer who had arrived in St. Louis in 1904 from South Carolina. After her birth, supposedly in a cardboard box, Baker lived with her mother and sister in a slum on Lucas Street. Official records said a drummer named Eddie Carson was her father, but that fact is far from certain. What's more certain is that McDonald and Carson formed a song-and-dance act, which took hold in a town known for its ragtime music.

Baker learned the music scene as she witnessed firsthand one of the darkest events of the St. Louis area's history: the bloody East St. Louis race riots of 1917. Horrified, she left St. Louis with a vaudeville troupe at thirteen, married a man named Willie Baker in Philadelphia two years later, and left him when she had a chance to work in New York. She kept the name Baker. At the age of nineteen, she grabbed at an offer to receive $250 a week to be part of a show in Paris.

In Paris, she shocked audiences as the bare-breasted star of the all-black *La Revue Nègre*. Sometimes wearing only a banana skirt, she sang and danced for titillated audiences who wanted more than the jazz brought by American soldiers during World War I. In Austria, students inveighed against "the appearance on the stage of any Negro artist," while members of parliament argued whether Baker should perform in their country. The issue wasn't race, said an Austrian parliamentarian, but the fact she appeared on stage "dressed only in a postage stamp."

Baker consorted in lavish outfits with the silk-stocking set and dwelt in a chateau with a bed supposedly used by Marie Antoinette. But when she returned to New York in 1935 to perform with the Ziegfeld Follies, she wrote, "If I want to make a telephone call in the street, I am still a Negress." In Manhattan, she appeared at a gala party for composer George Gershwin after the premiere of *Porgy and Bess* and left for St. Louis the next day to see her mother. Back in France in 1937, she married French industrialist Jean Lyon in a ceremony at the Paris City Hall. By marrying Lyon, she became a French citizen.

After German tanks overran France in 1940, Baker used her position to extract information from German officers she saw at parties. She smuggled that intelligence to the Allies on trips out of France. Details were on invisible ink written on sheet music and on photographs pinned inside her dress. She also worked in soup kitchens, bought food and toys for those in need, and later entertained Allied troops. For this, she received the Medal of the Resistance in 1946.

Baker kept dancing, singing, and speaking out after the war. "To me, for years, St. Louis represented a city of fear, humiliation, misery, and terror—a city where in the eyes of the white man, a Negro should know his place, and had better stay in it," she told a gathering at St. Louis's Kiel Auditorium in 1952. That year in Argentina, she told those mourning the death of the iconic Eva Peron that "the United States is not a free country," and that African Americans were treated "like dogs."

In the 1950s, Baker hit on her own way to fight racism by adopting twelve children from various parts of the world. It was her way of showing that children from anywhere can live together. High bills forced her to go on more tours to make expenses. But all did not end well. Her demanding nature drove away her fourth husband. Two of the children went to live with him. In 1968, deep in debt, she lost a castle she bought after the war for her children. She died of a cerebral hemorrhage in 1975 at the age of sixty-eight, within days of a performance in Paris to support her children. Born into poverty in St. Louis, Josephine Baker went on to influence the world.

# Dick Gregory: Laughing at Racism

**M**en who got shoeshines from Dick Gregory would say he was a happy kid who smiled as he caught your quarter. "Then he ran off and bought himself a Twinkie Cupcake, a bottle of Pepsi-Cola, and a pocketful of caramels," said Gregory's 1964 autobiography, with the grating title *Nigger*. "You didn't know that was his dinner. And you never followed him home." He was one of many boys born in North St. Louis whose lives seemed destined for failure. But in his case, he rose to make $7,500 a week in the early 1960s telling jokes about what it was like to be black in white America. "Segregation is not all that bad," he'd tell black and white audiences. "Have you ever heard of a collision where the people in the back of the bus got hurt?" And then, when he was at the top, he turned to a life advocating for people who grew up like he did.

Gregory started telling jokes soon after he was born in 1932 to a single mother. One of six kids who lived with their mother at 1803

North Taylor Avenue, he saw humor as a way to ease his hunger. When he went to Sumner High School, he learned he could get a hot shower after practice if he joined the track team. He went on to win the all-state mile, half-mile, and cross-country races. As he became a star on the track, he also led his first civil rights march. As a high school senior in 1951, he led a march to protest overcrowding at Vashon, Washington, and Sumner, the three high schools for African American students. When the St. Louis Board of Education refused to provide money for new buildings, students led by Gregory

marched to the Board of Education's building downtown and blocked its door.

The march may have gotten headlines, but Gregory's prowess on the track led to a scholarship to Southern Illinois University Carbondale. His time at Carbondale was interrupted by two years in the army. In the military, he won talent shows for his jokes. Back at SIU, he got accolades for his comedy and his skill on the track. But he concluded that a degree didn't matter for a black man, and he quit school three hours shy of getting his business administration degree. He headed to Chicago, where he worked days as a postal worker and nights honing his skills as a comedian.

The comedy work didn't help him move to the middle class. He made ten dollars a night and worked three nights a week. When he asked for a two-dollar-a-night raise, his boss fired him. "I had a single room in a basement. I got so far behind they were going to put me out," he recalled later. He did his own laundry, "and you'd be surprised how clean a suit can stay when you can't afford to have it cleaned." Then one day he walked into a booking office at the same time that a call came in from the Playboy Club. It was a great opportunity except for one thing. Southerners made up the audience, and they'd been drinking. No matter. They loved him, and before long, he was on *Tonight Starring Jack Paar.*

He was headed for the top when he made a detour to spend time fighting for civil rights and to run as a minor candidate for president in the 1968 presidential election. "[Gregory] had no chance of winning, and he knew that," St. Louis North Side alderman Freeman Bosley Sr. told the *Post-Dispatch* in 2008. "He did it to heighten awareness that change had to come. Had it not been for Dick Gregory, Barack Obama would not be as far as he is today," said Bosley, who went to Sumner with Gregory. Some of Gregory's campaigns were common to the civil rights movement. Others were off the path, as he became a vegetarian and claimed to beat cancer with nontraditional methods. He participated in numerous fasts, including one for forty days to protest child molestation charges against singer Michael Jackson. Jackson was acquitted in 2005.

Over time, St. Louisans showed their respect for Gregory with significant honors. Southern Illinois University Carbondale awarded him an honorary degree. St. Louis's Wagoner Place was renamed Dick Gregory Place, while Kinloch's Winton Street got the name Dick Gregory Drive. In 1995, a star with his name on it was added to the St. Louis Walk of Fame on Delmar Boulevard. As good as that may be, the best honor might be the fulfillment of a promise made to his mother in his 1964 autobiography: "When we're through, Momma, there won't be any niggers anymore."

# Father Dismas Clark: Priest to the Unwanted

Ever the ex-con's best friend, Father Charles Dismas Clark had a surefire way to ensure that his former jailbirds stayed out of prison. When a bad guy tried to bring an ex-con back to a life of crime, Clark alerted his friends in the mob. The bad guy stayed away. A conversation with Clark might include the observation, "I know eight or nine ways to kill you without making a sound." Why shouldn't he know? He palled around enough with people familiar with such things. Such were the unorthodox ways of a St. Louis priest who spent his life fighting for a second chance for those coming out of prison. After he died in 1963, six former convicts—a murderer and five thieves—bore his coffin to the grave. When people talked about him, they called him the Hoodlum Priest.

Clark took the name Dismas from the repentant thief granted sainthood by Jesus as both were dying on side-by-side crosses. His choice of friends might seem odd for a Jesuit priest. His biggest supporter was Morris Shenker, a Jewish lawyer who purportedly defended mobsters. Shenker provided the backing for Dismas House, a pioneering halfway house for ex-convicts.

One of thirteen children of a coal miner in Decatur, Illinois, Clark chose a religious vocation after an encounter at seventeen with a priest who told him that the greatest joy in life comes from helping others. He was ordained in 1932 and started his ministry to former prisoners four years later. He learned what made convicts tick and what made them hurt. He counseled them and found them jobs. Clark said he wanted to be the one to help them at their hour of need. "Have you ever seen a man's eyes empty of hope?" he said. Lawyers and prosecutors hid when he showed up at court. They knew Clark wanted to say a word for his "unfortunate boys."

Police, parole, and prison officers were well acquainted with him, although many considered him a troublemaker. Even some of his church superiors tut-tutted him. He fought back by sharply criticizing those in business, the educational system, and the courts for their failure to do what they should do with convicts. "Judges are worse than criminals," he would say. "A lawyer who can't make a living gets himself appointed judge. What can you expect from our courts?" But he also found support in the press and among civic leaders, which he would need in the biggest project of his life.

At the end of the 1950s, Clark started looking for a building big enough to house former offenders while they adjusted to life on the outside. Today that's a common practice in halfway houses all over the country. But back in the late 1950s, it was new. Owners of fifteen buildings turned him down. A sixteenth offered to sell him an abandoned ninety-year-old school building at 905 Cole Street in North St. Louis for forty thousand dollars—big money in those days. Clark told Shenker about his idea for Dismas House. Shenker made the down payment, guaranteed the loan, and paid the interest. For the first six months of Dismas House's operation, Shenker wouldn't allow anyone else to provide money. Then Shenker raised $73,000 from friends. Dismas House took off. As many as sixty residents at a time spent about two months getting used to living on the outside and seeking a job.

News about Dismas House spread. One person who learned about it was actor Don Murray. In town to promote a movie, Murray invited Clark to his hotel room. The priest amazed Murray with tales about the ex-cons he'd encountered. As a result, Murray gave Dismas House ten thousand dollars for the right to use Clark's story in a movie. From that came the 1961 movie *The Hoodlum Priest*. Shot in St. Louis, it received critical acclaim but was panned by some locally. The *Globe-Democrat* attacked it for promoting a mentality that pities criminals and giving St. Louis a bad rap. But Clark contended that *The Hoodlum Priest* would bring positive publicity to St. Louis by noting what St. Louis did for ex-convicts.

There was much to praise. When Clark died unexpectedly at sixty-one in August 1963, more than two thousand former offenders had gone through the program. Around 95 percent of those didn't return to jail. Halfway houses were well on their way to being a national movement. Shenker said Clark could be hard to understand and that many disagreed with him. But he contended that the priest was a man who dedicated himself to people that society wanted to forget.

# Percy Green: Master of Outrage

With throngs of ravishing debutantes dressed in stunning blue, white, purple, and red evening gowns, the Veiled Prophet Ball has been the annual celebration of life for St. Louis's privileged class since 1878. The ball and an accompanying Veiled Prophet Parade long entranced St. Louisans, regardless of class. But in the 1960s, a civil rights organization called ACTION concluded that the Veiled Prophet organization was a central social group for the heads of local corporations that denied

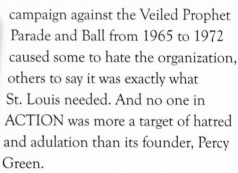

jobs to African Americans. ACTION's campaign against the Veiled Prophet Parade and Ball from 1965 to 1972 caused some to hate the organization, others to say it was exactly what St. Louis needed. And no one in ACTION was more a target of hatred and adulation than its founder, Percy Green.

Many hated Green for the headline-grabbing tactics he used as a civil rights organizer. Others say the street theater he performed was just the approach needed in the fight to end discrimination and open up jobs to African Americans. The *Post-Dispatch* called Green "St. Louis's most outrageous man." The conservative *Globe-Democrat* called him "St. Louis's non-stop racial agitator." But that wasn't what this son of a near South Side packinghouse worker wanted to do when he went to work for McDonnell Aircraft Corp. (later McDonnell-Douglas and Boeing) in the 1950s. "I was just a regular person who was living what was considered a normal life for a black person, doing what the average young person would be doing," he said. Then something happened.

It started after a coworker suggested he attend the Sunday meetings of a civil rights group called the Congress of Racial Equality (CORE). In discussions at the meetings, a man named Eugene Tournour talked about the white power structure in corporations, churches, and other institutions in St. Louis. As Green puts it, he "discovered that black folks were not in the predicament that black folks were in by choice. There had to be something that was responsible." The talk convinced Green that something was wrong and that he had to be a part of the changes of the turbulent 1960s.

In August 1963, Green and CORE led demonstrations against what they saw as racial discrimination in hiring at a local bank, the Jefferson Bank & Trust. Then they turned their attention toward jobs at the federally funded construction of the Gateway Arch. MacDonald Construction Co., the prime contractor for the project, claimed there weren't any qualified black workers. The activists put the squeeze on MacDonald and planned something big. On July 14, 1964, Green and white activist Richard Daly walked onto the worksite past workers eating lunch. They scurried up ladders on the north side and climbed to 125 feet. Green thought the sensational protest shouldn't affect his job, but it did. About six weeks after the Gateway Arch incident, McDonnell let him go for "workforce reduction." He sued under the Civil Rights Act of 1964. The case went all the way to the Supreme Court. At the end, the court made it easier to prove workplace discrimination. But Green didn't get his job back. That personal experience of losing his job affected him deeply.

In 1965, Green became the leader of a new civil rights group. Called ACTION, it focused on a variety of disruptions, often against big business in St. Louis. People always remember the group for what it did against one local institution, the Veiled Prophet Ball. In 1965, the group organized protests against the parade and ball, and in 1972 it struck at the center of the ball's mystique. A woman in an evening gown sneaked behind the Veiled Prophet, snatched the covering from him, and tossed it away. The veil was soon returned, but not before everyone knew it was a Monsanto executive vice president named Tom K. Smith.

ACTION disbanded in 1985, but Green kept fighting, getting arrested, making enemies and friends, and generally doing outrageous things. In 1993, he was named to lead the city's process to certify businesses that meet the city's requirements for being minority- and women-owned. In 2001, Mayor Francis Slay eliminated Green's job and his office and combined it with another one. At the time, Green said the firing was a sham. He now worries that more unqualified front companies really owned by whites will slip through. Today, at eighty-one, Green continues his work. Many institutions that once opposed him are now strong backers. When the city celebrated the fiftieth anniversary of the completion of the Gateway Arch in 2015, many told the story of Green's climb up the side. The CityArchRiver 2015 Foundation, which organized the drive to refurbish the Arch grounds, gave him an award for his courage in making the climb. Looking back, it's easy to see that sometimes it's best to do the outrageous thing.

# Larry Rice: Stubborn for Good

**N**ot everybody would look forward to spending a frigid night shivering in a cardboard box next to St. Louis City Hall. But it does help a person understand what the homeless go through all the time, says St. Louis gadfly and homeless advocate Larry Rice. Rice, the founder and president of St. Louis's New Life Evangelistic Center, has frequently found himself outside on cold nights, seeking homeless people who refused to come to his downtown shelter. He's also spent all night outside, including in protests in the 1980s, when he and others tried to sleep around St. Louis City Hall. But inside a cardboard box, he never could rest.

Rice's son Chris Rice remembers sleeping outside city hall around 1986, when he was about twelve. "I remember it being bitterly cold," said Chris Rice, who now does administration and pastoral work at New Life. "I remember feeling like I couldn't feel my fingers and toes," no matter how he tried to retain as much body heat as possible inside his cardboard box. When he sees homeless people losing their fingers and toes from frostbite, he empathizes more than he did before. "Doing this causes you to identify with people," Larry Rice said. Many on his staff don't need to do anything to identify with the homeless because they've lived on the streets.

It also may explain why Larry Rice has a reputation for not going along. For decades, he's been on the wrong side of St. Louis mayors, downtown developers, the Missouri Public Service Commission, officials in Cape Girardeau, and a bevy of others. A Texas native, Rice came to St. Louis to attend Concordia Seminary in St. Louis. He left the seminary because of religious turmoil on campus and was ordained in 1971 by an interdenominational church called Calvary Temple in Fort Wayne, Indiana. The next year, he started New Life in a trailer in Wellston. Since 1976, the ministry has been in its downtown shelter, at 1411 Locust Street. Publicity about the organization focuses on its downtown shelter, but the group also runs shelters in Potosi, Van Buren, Columbia, and Springfield, Missouri; provides job training and other services for the homeless; and has several television and radio stations.

At times, Rice's protests have been opportunities for humor. In 1989, New Life got publicity after Rice gave the okay to put down a buffalo that wandered away during a storm from a farm the group owned near Jefferson City. The organization, which was fighting redevelopment legislation that Rice claimed expanded eminent domain powers, used some meat from the animal to serve state legislators free buffalo burger meals. Hungry lawmakers were told not to let lobbyists "buffalo" them. It was a light moment in a push that saw New Life criticized for heavy-handed tactics. To show opposition, Rice and others posted a "public notice" on the state capitol door of senate Republican Minority Leader Tom McCarthy of Chesterfield declaring his office blighted. Then some of Rice's supporters planted a similar notice at the home of McCarthy's mother in Chesterfield. McCarthy said the episode frightened his mother and condemned it as "rank thuggery." Rice said he regretted the incident, but added that many experience blight every day without equal protection of the law.

Rice has also come under criticism for what's happened around its downtown shelter. Residents of that area have long claimed that the homeless who use the shelter at night hurt the surrounding neighborhood with panhandling, drug use, littering, loitering, and crime. Mayor Francis Slay has frequently campaigned against the center. Bill Siedhoff, the city's retired human services director, praises Rice for raising public awareness of the homeless. But he favors moving the homeless from temporary shelters to long-term housing as soon as possible. "Just sheltering people is not the remedy," he said. Larry Rice likes to give the blues to certain public officials, Siedhoff said. "I think he enjoys that." Chris Rice agrees there's a need for permanent housing but said St. Louis doesn't provide for those who need emergency shelters. The city's policies have left a large number of people on the streets, he said.

But Larry Rice says that people who speak up for the homeless can expect opposition. "We'd do whatever we can to keep before the public the issue of the homeless," he said. Chris Rice said his father is following Christian principles that require people to help the poor. But he agrees that part of what causes Larry Rice to act as he does comes from his personality. "He has a very strong personality. He can be stubborn for good," Chris Rice said. "In a lot of ways, we're always going to be the fly in the ointment."

# Randy Grim: He Speaks for the Dogs

B
urned into the mind of Randy Grim is the memory of a
father who beat him and the eyes of a dog who was abused
as badly as he was. It's awful, but that memory set Grim on
a path to improve the lives of thousands of stray dogs in St. Louis
and the nation. His quest led him to set up an organization meant
to get stray animals off St. Louis's streets and into the homes of
loving owners. Stray Rescue has virtually ended the practice of
euthanizing animals picked up on St. Louis streets, has taken over
much of the city's animal rescue operations, and has vastly reduced
the number of strays on the city's streets.

Grim is out of his element when he sits behind his desk on
the second floor of his office at Stray Rescue's building on the

far end of downtown to
talk about the work he
started. Paintings of dogs
cover the wall behind
him. A rambunctious
dog named Miss
Wagner, or Miss Wags,
is by his side, ever
ready to coat the face
of visitors with kisses.
It seems comfortable,
but Grim would rather
be out on the streets
rescuing animals. Most
days he is. He has the
title of founder, but he would rather just consider himself another
worker in a nonprofit meant to help animals.

Born in 1962 in Washington, D.C., he looked for ways to get away from his abusive father. "My escape when I was a little kid was to steal the tuna and milk and feed the sewer cats, and then they became my friend," he said. One winter day, he went out with his brother and found a bone-thin Irish setter lying in the snow. "We each took an end of its legs and carried him home." They made a fire in the fireplace and placed the dog next to it. He looked into the dog's eyes and saw fear, but not any fear. "I knew its fear all too well," Grim said. It was his own. He connected with the animal. From then on, he was compelled to go out and rescue helpless animals. "Every time I rescue a dog, I save a little piece of me. It's almost what I've been born to do."

Grim did something about his feelings after he grew up, moved to St. Louis, and found a place to live in Lafayette Square. The neighborhood was nothing like it is today. "There were packs of dogs everywhere. There were tons of strays," he said. He set about rescuing as many as he could. He would use fishing poles with chicken at the end of a string to entice them to a place where he could capture them.

Grim recruited others to help him and took his passion to a new level in 1998, when he founded Stray Rescue. With ten thousand dollars from his life savings, he bought a building in Lafayette Square. The media took note, both locally and nationally. Writer Melinda Roth spent weeks picking up dogs with Grim in 1999 for a profile in the *Riverfront Times*, then developed it into the 2004 book, *The Man Who*

*Talks to Dogs.* Profiles in such outlets as Animal Planet and *National Geographic* added to the attention, as did a couple of books he wrote about dogs.

As Grim's fame grew, local officials started depending on Stray Rescue. In 2010, the group opened its shelter at 2320 Pine St. to replace the abysmal old city pound on Gasconade Street. The new building is bright, with a lobby, kennels, a veterinarian's office and operating room, and a lounge where potential owners can meet dogs. The organization rescues about three thousand dogs and adopts out twenty-six hundred of them a year. The rest go into foster homes.

People all over the country may know about him, but Grim spends as much of his time as possible out rescuing, just as he did in those days in Lafayette Square. He doesn't always like what he finds. One day, he rescued an emaciated Labrador mix in North St. Louis. It weighed about sixteen and a half pounds, about a third of its normal weight. "I remember one woman who was saying 'Thank God you got here.'" The woman, a neighbor, had watched the dog slowly wasting away. "That was breaking my heart," Grim said. At Stray Rescue, the pooch quickly got its wag back. He senses that his work has brought a change in the community. "It's not me anymore," he said. "It's an army. It's a community. Probably the biggest honor in the world is knowing it's not me anymore."

# Eric Brende: Doing Better by Doing Without

**E**ric Brende doesn't ride a horse and buggy around the South Side like the Amish might. But Brende and his wife, Mary, raised their three kids without a car, television, Xbox, or internet. They're one with the Amish and similar groups in believing that a simple life of saying no to many modern comforts is the better way. They believe St. Louis is an ideal place to pursue that simple life because it's designed for walkers.

Growing up in Minnesota and Topeka, Kansas, Brende was accustomed to using anything that was new. It wasn't always for the good, he said. When the family got an automatic dishwasher, more dishes seemed to pile up. He studied this at Yale University, when he took courses in the history of technology while pursuing an English degree. To fulfill requirements for the Massachusetts Institute of Technology's Program for Science, Technology, and

Society, the Brendes lived with a religious community similar to the Amish in the early 1990s. That led him to write *Better Off*, a 2004 book about the community. The group's use of technology was based on whether it promotes or detracts from the solidarity of the group, Brende said. Here was a better way, he thought. Said Brende: "You can only increase the radius of contact by diluting the quality of contact with your next door neighbors."

In the late 1990s, they continued their life of holding technology at arm's length by opening a bed and breakfast in Hermann, Missouri. Brende made money taking tourists around Hermann with a foot-powered rickshaw. They generally used a kerosene lamp and a wood stove rather than a furnace and only turned on the air conditioner when customers stayed for the night. They rarely used their car. "It was a very idyllic place," Brende said. Nonetheless, the couple decided in 2003 to continue that lifestyle in St. Louis's McKinley Heights neighborhood.

Brende is convinced their choice of lifestyle is easier in the city because everything is closer together. When great restaurants and live entertainment are within bicycle range, TV or DVDs aren't necessary, he believes. When they must go further, they've accepted rides and once even took an Uber car. They've also rented a car to make a trip to Kansas City.

They only use air conditioning when company is in town and eschew kitchen conveniences like microwaves or toasters. They do have a gas stove, electric lights, a landline phone, and a word processing computer. Brende sometimes takes a flash drive to a library and sends documents by e-mail. When he wrote *Better Off*, his publisher made him get an e-mail address. He uses e-mail to keep up with friends. But he won't surf the web, and he absolutely won't go on Facebook. Brende uses his rickshaw to drive people around Cardinals games, Mardi Gras, and special events. The Brendes sell handmade soap at Soulard Market.

That lifestyle is easier within a self-sustaining Amish community, Brende notes, but harder when nobody else lives that way. The family adjusted by living with people who use the modern conveniences. They live without air conditioning, using older methods of dealing with heat, like opening the upper sashes of upper windows and choosing a home with ten-foot ceilings and shade on the east and west sides. To connect with friends, they organize events at their house so they don't have to travel. In exchange for bars of soap, Mary Brende gets rides to a book group that meets in Brentwood. From his experience, Brende says his way of life enabled him to spend less time working and more time relaxing.

The three Brende kids were part of this experiment, even if they sometimes complained that they didn't have cell phones and television. Hans and Evan homeschooled through eighth grade and attended St. Louis University High School. Both biked four miles each way to high school. Evan, a recent St. Louis University High graduate, is a composer and performed key roles in his school's plays. He'll attend Catholic University in Washington, D.C., in the fall of 2016. Hans graduated from the University of Tulsa after winning the school's Presidential Scholarship. Taking a different path, Hans took to computers in high school. He's in charge of technology at a start-up company. Anna homeschooled through high school and studies music therapy at Catholic University. "They grew up with very long attention spans and physically fit," Brende said. They sometimes complained that they didn't have things others did. But Hans once told Brende he wouldn't change anything. Nonetheless, Brende expects his kids will live the modern life once they leave home. Those wanting details can call Anna and Hans on their smartphones.

# Cbabi Bayoc: Masterpiece for the Dads

C aricature artist Cbabi Bayoc once did an album cover for Prince. Over the years, he's had such clients as MCA Records, Anheuser-Busch, the *St. Louis Post-Dispatch*, Coca-Cola, and New Line Cinema. He's done the covers of magazines and children's books. But his biggest project so far has been an effort to use his talents to celebrate African American fathers. The Shaw neighborhood resident started in 2012, intending to do one painting a day for a year. It actually took two years and nearly two months. When he finished, he got out champagne and celebrated with friends. He had good reason for his dedication for the collection of paintings he called "365 Days with Dad." Said Bayoc: "I want to push the idea that there are responsible black men that are taking care of their children."

Whatever Cbabi Bayoc does and for whatever reason, his paintings are full of color, with characters' features delightfully extended. Bayoc said he loves turning nothing into something. "People have so many unique features. Being able to exaggerate and make 'em look like somebody is pretty cool." Born Clifford Miskell Jr., he decided to be an artist while he was studying for his bachelor's degree from Grambling State University in Grambling, Louisiana. He took the first name Cbabi (Kuh-BOB-bi), an acronym for "Creative Black Artist Battling Ignorance." After he married his wife, Reine, in 1998, they came up with the last name "Bayoc." It means "Blessed African Youth of Creativity."

His artwork is on the walls of the SweetArt Bakery, which he and his wife own in the Shaw neighborhood. He uses it as a place to show off his artwork, while she displays her skill in preparing traditional and vegan baked yummy things and a vegetarian lunch. It makes for great eating, but what he really sunk his teeth into as an artist is the project to paint 365 black fathers. "I've always wanted to think of doing a body of work, but I never could," he said. "I just hadn't seen any dad images. So I knew there was a need

for it." His wife suggested making fathers the subject, and so he did. Customers e-mailed pictures, and the paintings could depict fathers doing anything. Not everybody liked the idea that all of his subjects would be black. "I got bombarded with the idea that fatherhood is universal, and you should paint all cultures, and I said 'You are absolutely right, but those who don't have dads, they need to know that they can be a dad when they become an adult.'"

He set to work on the project, not with splashes of color, but tidal waves of blue, red, brown, and green. In one painting of the collection, a smiling dad bows down to pose next to his preschool daughter. In another, a father helps his young daughter onto a horse. A third shows a dad all grins as he makes space on his lap for his daughter, while others show kids welcoming their dads home from work with a big squeeze and riding atop their dad's shoulders. And in one more, a dad is in the hospital with his brand-new child.

While most of his paintings are joyful, Bayoc put a serious face on a painting he did after the shooting of Michael Brown by a Ferguson police officer on August 9, 2014. Painted across the street from the burnt-out QT in Ferguson, the artwork showed a black man wearing a T-shirt with the words "RIP Son." A boy hugs him, and another stands in front of him. The man is meant to signify Michael Brown's father and Tracy Martin, the father of Florida teenager Trayvon Martin, who was killed by a former neighborhood watch volunteer. "We may not be producing anything now, because we've been so consumed by what is going on," Bayoc told *Art in America* magazine right after the shooting. "But a lot of art is going to come out of this."

The 365 Days with Dad artwork has numerous fans. Local public radio station KWMU covered Bayoc's collection extensively. He's selling a calendar and prints based on the series. He did a TED talk on his project at Harris-Stowe State University. The talk was part of a national effort to have people give speeches on technology, entertainment, and design. He's given the same message at St. Louis University and at other schools. "Some people say they notice dads more now," he said. "I've gotten e-mails from people all over the place." People still ask him to paint dads of all races. But among his daughter and two sons, the reaction was more ho-hum. "I've been painting since they were born, so it's not new to them."

# Daniel "Boone" Fuller: The Vigil of Daniel "Boone" Fuller

S t. Louisans were living in fear, and cold, hard statistics showed the reason why. In the first half of 2014, police recorded sixty-five homicides within the city. In the first half of 2015, ninety-two people were killed. The number of killings shot up from six in June 2014 to twenty-two in June 2015. That was too many for Daniel "Boone" Fuller. So in the summer of 2015, he announced that he would live between two billboards in North St. Louis and wouldn't come down until murders stopped for seven days. What happened next, he said, "raised awareness of the need for people to get involved to stop this senseless violence."

Fuller has a way of attracting attention. His company, AdUnity Media, sold space on one hundred billboards showing the face of Muhammad to Pamela Geller's controversial American Freedom Defense Initiative. He said he came up with the idea for a vigil through his business. Most of the five hundred small billboards his company has are in high-crime areas affected by murders. He's gotten to know property owners and neighbors as he's slapped new paper on those signs. "You see death and destruction and murder every single day on the news and in real life," he said. He knew he had to do something. But what?

He started with a contest for the best design for billboards with the best anti-bullying, anti-violence, and pro-community messages. It garnered lots of interest, but it didn't change the murder rates. Then he decided he would camp out in the space between two of his back-to-back billboards until there wasn't a murder in St. Louis for a week. He chose a location at Washington Boulevard and Sarah Street, not far from Delmar Boulevard, which many consider the divide between white and black St. Louis. Moving only from the living space between the billboards to a raised exercise area on a mobile billboard he'd trucked in, he estimates he didn't touch ground about 90 percent of the time. He arranged to do all his company's business by cell phone and started his vigil on his fiftieth birthday, July 9.

The first weekend, the owners of a soul food restaurant put out a mobile barbecue pit on the site. The restaurant owner, who also owned the property where the billboards were located, brought his whole family and camped out there the first weekend. About twenty people stayed overnight the first night. Two women from a nearby church brought in holy oil to anoint his feet and sprinkle around the property. Some of the curious and well-wishers included politicians like former mayor Freeman Bosley Jr. and State Senator Jamila Nasheed. Others were relatives or friends of murder victims.

But some weren't quite as friendly. One day, a woman approached him and said he needed to get out of there because he didn't belong there. "Get off the billboard, you cracker white devil," she said. As she chased him on the exercise area, he kicked a large rock he'd laid down to stabilize the plywood floor and severely hurt his foot. Friends told him he needed to seek medical attention, even if it meant briefly breaking his vigil. Finally, after several days, he drove to the emergency room at Barnes-Jewish

Hospital one night at 11 p.m. Doctors confirmed that the foot was broken and that the whole foot below the ankle was severely infected. They gave him antibiotics, put the foot in a special boot, and told him to go easy on it. His four-hour absence to seek treatment represented the only time he left his temporary home during the vigil. As the effort continued, he was frequently interviewed by phone, both by local reporters and those far away. To those who offered support, he said, "Don't root for me. Root for St. Louis to go seven days without a murder."

But that wasn't happening. There might be one, two, or three days without a murder, but nothing approaching seven days. But following a homicide on July 26, the killings seemed to stop. Excitement grew on the sixth day, August 1, as there were no murders. On August 2, the seventh day, he was ready to declare victory, when reporters came to his encampment and told him that there had been another killing. There hadn't been seven full days without a homicide. Fuller insists this is quibbling and that what

happened was close enough. "I think it was an accomplishment, and I reached my goals," said Fuller, who ended his vigil that day. For him, this was personal. The murders happened where he did business. He wanted to do something, even if it meant spending twenty-six days camped out between two billboards.

# Rev. Kenneth McKoy: Walking to Stop the Killing

For the Reverend Kenneth McKoy, the scenario has played out too many times in recent years. He befriends some promising teenager, talks to him about college, and then gets the call. The teenager is the victim of yet another shooting. "You're not prepared to bury a child at seventeen who you baptized at fourteen," said McKoy, who is pastor of the Progressive African Methodist Episcopal Zion Church in northwestern St. Louis. Since McKoy organized the church in 2012, he's officiated at six funerals for victims of gunshots in that violent area. His own son was shot four times but survived. He wearied of seeing so many mothers and grandmothers crying at funerals.

Some people might run away from that kind of violence, but McKoy walked toward it. Today he spends the late-night hours

leading a group walking around some of the bloodiest parts of St. Louis. He probably would have been safer had he remained as pastor of Blackwell Chapel African Methodist Episcopal Zion Church in Webster Groves. But God had other plans.

As a teenager, McKoy moved with his mother from Washington, D.C., to North Carolina to get away from the crime. He graduated from Shaw University in Raleigh, North Carolina, and was ordained a deacon of the African Methodist Episcopal Church in 1984 and an elder in 1987. He got some surprises when his church work brought him to St. Louis in 1985. "When I got here, St. Louis was very, very violent," McKoy said. "Drive-by shootings, and I didn't know enough to be afraid." Things got less violent but then got bad again in recent years.

As he saw unpleasant changes, he served as the executive director of the community organization Missouri Acorn from 2002 to 2006. "For the first time in my life, I connected the two, social activism and the church," McKoy said. The experience opened his eyes to issues around class and racism and taught him how to organize in the community. Then in 2009, a young man he knew went missing. McKoy was sitting with the man's grandmother when she got a call that police had found his body. He had been brutally murdered. "It was overwhelming to the family. It was overwhelming to me." Hundreds of young people came to the funeral, some talking revenge. He felt he had to do more. In 2012, he got permission to organize the Progressive African Methodist Episcopal Zion Church as a way to be in the city.

The killings continued, and in August 2014 he found himself at the protests against the shooting of Michael Brown by a Ferguson police officer. He was there both as a demonstrator and to ensure no young person would get hurt. "I remember thinking how many black men have been murdered since this whole Ferguson uprising," McKoy said. "That's when I just decided that I'm going to dedicate the rest of my life to street ministry." With that decision made, McKoy and some other friends from the clergy started their walks in May 2015.

The late-night walkers varied in number from seven to more than thirty and have included a motley collection of conservative evangelicals, atheists, Black Panthers, Black Nationalists, Ferguson protesters, Harvard grads, and a Republican from St. Charles. To make the walks as safe as possible, they always start with prayer and don bright yellow safety vests. Members of the clergy always wear their collars. But that didn't make them completely safe. At the beginning, McKoy received two or three death threats a week. He discovered who was making the threats and arranged a meeting. The threats stopped after they understood he wasn't working with the police to get them locked up.

Walkers bring food for the homeless they encounter, and McKoy carries a wooden cross on Good Friday. One night, a young man started walking with the group. After a short time, the man stepped back, pulled out a nine millimeter pistol, and told McKoy he planned to kill somebody that night. McKoy hugged the man and asked him if he had any children. When the man said he did, McKoy asked him what the son would do without a father. The man canceled his plans. Several months later, the man ran into McKoy, gave him a hug, and said McKoy had saved his life. In their first year, McKoy estimates, the walks stopped three murders from happening, and with it, three funerals, along with bitter tears from three families. Three would-be murderers had another chance at living to help their own families. That's not enough to halt a crime wave, but it's enough to keep the Reverend Kenneth McKoy walking at night.

# POLITICOS

# Thomas Hart Benton: Guns, Politics, and a Dying Man's Vote

I n thirty years representing Missouri in the US Senate, Thomas Hart Benton was known as one of the greatest orators of the pre–Civil War US Congress. Some say he was the greatest politician St. Louis ever produced. He may have been the most explosive, both in speech and in his use of a gun. Before he began his thirty-year career in the Senate, he killed a man in a duel in St. Louis and almost killed a future president. After he reached the upper house of Congress, though, he limited his fire to explosive oratory aimed at his political opponents.

Born in North Carolina in 1782, Benton showed his fiery ways early. As a student at the University of North Carolina at Chapel Hill, he nearly shot another student. He started practicing law, moved west to Tennessee, and was elected to that state's legislature. With the coming of the War of 1812, he volunteered to serve in the Tennessee State Militia under the popular Andrew Jackson. Bad feeling grew between Benton and Jackson that led to a duel in which Benton shot Jackson in the left arm. So strong was the enmity against Benton after the shooting that he moved to St. Louis.

Benton developed a reputation as a lawyer with a sharp tongue and as a newspaper editor who called for statehood. He gained friends and enemies. In 1817, Benton found himself in a duel over his alleged use of the epithet "puppy," when an attorney claimed Benton couldn't vote because he hadn't paid his poll tax. Benton fatally shot the attorney, Charles Lucas, in a contest on Bloody Island in the middle of the Mississippi River.

In spite of the incident, Benton became a main contender when the first General Assembly of the state of Missouri convened in 1820 to name the first US senators of the new state. Benton was one vote short of victory. That vote came from Daniel Ralls, who was on his deathbed in the hotel where the vote was being taken. Ralls asked four large men to pick up each corner of his bed and carry him down the stairs to the meeting room. He voted for Benton and then was carried back upstairs to die.

In the Senate, Benton gained prominence under his former nemesis, Andrew Jackson. When doctors removed Benton's old bullet from his arm, Jackson jokingly tried to give it back to him. Benton refused. Along with Jackson, Benton wanted a sound currency based on gold and silver instead of state bank "rag" money and national bank notes. He promoted land grants to settlers, fought for the annexation of Texas, and battled for a railroad to the Pacific Ocean and for westward expansion. But at least in fiction, he was a letdown for one boy. In *The Adventures of Tom Sawyer*, the book's namesake anxiously awaits the arrival of Benton in Hannibal. He is disappointed to discover that Benton wasn't twenty-five feet tall.

Many in Missouri had that impression of Benton's stature, but it was slavery that brought him down. He owned slaves himself, but he opposed spreading the institution into the territories. In 1849, he fought pro-slavery forces that wanted to prevent him from having another term and encountered catcalls when he took his fight to areas where opposition was the greatest. In 1851, the state assembly turned him out of his senate seat.

Benton rejected talk about running for president in 1852. Instead, he served a term in Congress and wasn't reelected. He made a failed run for governor in 1856, hit the lecture circuit, and wrote his memoirs. When he died in 1858, as much as a quarter of the city's population of 160,000 turned out for events connected with his funeral. Ten years later, thousands more turned out for the dedication of a statue of Benton in Lafayette Park. No ordinary garb or stature would suffice for this likeness. Instead, his figure is twice life-size, in the garb of a Roman emperor—almost enough to impress Tom Sawyer.

# Bryan Mullanphy: The Eccentric Philanthropist

The hardware store clerk must have been aghast. He'd never received an order like this, but, then again, there never was an order-giver like Bryan Mullanphy. Three hundred razors, all at once, and these weren't Gillette Fusion Power Cartridges. They were straight razors, the kind sold in the stores of St. Louis before 1850. The eccentric millionaire buyer dispensed the cutting instruments to travelers passing through the young Gateway to the West. With them, the emigrants might starve when their wagons broke down in the middle of a Western desert, but they would do it with clean faces. "Some said," one observer wrote, "that Judge Mullanphy's eccentricity marred his usefulness, but it is a pity that the Almighty did not inflict such eccentricity on more persons. For here was a man of plenty who knew how to give things away."

Bryan Mullanphy was destined to wealth, if not oddball ways to distribute it. A lifelong bachelor, he was born in 1809 in Baltimore, the only son of John Mullanphy. An emigrant from Ireland, John Mullanphy came with his wife, Elizabeth, to St. Louis in 1804 and amassed a fortune as a merchant. Much of it he gave to others. With a portion, he established the Orphan Asylum of the Ladies of the Sacred Heart, and with another he started the St. Louis Mullanphy Hospital and imported members of the Sisters of Charity to run it. By the time he died in 1833, John

Mullanphy left a fortune estimated at the then-unheard-of sum of $5 to $6 million.

Bryan Mullanphy spent much of his youth at schools in France and England and returned well acquainted with music and literature and skilled in the law. But he did not impress his father, who cut him out of his will because of reckless behavior. Fortunately for Bryan, his sisters redivided his will when their father died to give him an equal portion. He became a judge and was elected to the board of aldermen and then mayor in 1847. As people in St. Louis came to know Bryan Mullanphy, they also came to know that here was a man who didn't do things the normal way.

Various stories exist telling how Mullanphy paid destitute widows to take care of his milk cows and to help themselves to whatever milk they produced. In one case, related by former mayor John F. Darby in his memoirs, *Personal Recollections of John F. Darby*, a woman from Illinois approached him with a cow and asked him to buy it. Mullanphy said he would buy it if his fence was finished, but it wasn't. He walked away and then came back. "I will give you the money for the cow now. Here it is," he said. "You take the cow back to your place in Illinois and keep her for me; and here is so much money to pay you for it." The woman never saw Bryan Mullanphy again. On another occasion, so the story went, he paid a poor family to live in and take care of a house he had bought and furnished.

Yet another story tells of how Mullanphy once spotted a destitute woman with six or seven children occupying a tenement he owned. She told him she had walked thirty miles to St. Louis, baby in arms, looking for work. When snow started falling, she decided there would be no harm in staying a few days. Mullanphy responded that she had broken the law and could be thrown in jail. To her begging, he responded that she must pay rent. She said she had no money at all. Then he said she could pay by doing sewing for a clothing store he owned. He arranged for a man who sold clothing to send her an ample amount of items to be sewn and to pay her twice as much as the jobs were worth. Mullanphy paid the man for the extra cost and provided the woman with furnishings. So he provided for the needs of many in St. Louis who were burdened with the kind of poverty that filled the books of Charles Dickens.

Mullanphy's work continued long after his death in 1851, when he left the huge sum of $500,000 to care for poor emigrants coming to St. Louis and travelers on their way west. From that start grew Travelers Aid International, an organization that provides help to stranded tourists in Travelers Aid Societies all over the United States. In St. Louis, the local group still bears the name Mullanphy Travelers Aid Society. More than 165 years after Mullanphy's death, the societies continue his work, although not with his unique style.

# Edward Gardner Lewis: Born for the Shell Game

I t was a big promise, but if you had ten friends and a buck, why not? The Progressive Watch Company offered to sell a book with ten coupons for a dollar. If you sold all ten coupons for a dime, you'd have your money back. If all ten buyers sent in their coupons with a dollar, they'd get a book, and you'd get a watch worth ten to twelve dollars. But nobody got any watches, and the post office decided in 1899 that the company was a fraud. All mail to the Progressive Watch Company came back stamped with the message "fraudulent." So ended another scheme by the man who soon would found University City: Edward Gardner Lewis.

The son of a New England Episcopal clergyman, Lewis attended Trinity College in Hartford, Connecticut, and quickly honed his unique way of doing business. He sold a tablet to fight the effects of nicotine, powder for sore feet, a cough remedy, and a mosquito repellent dabbed at the end of the nose. None worked.

Lewis was full of ideas when he came to St. Louis in the late 1890s. He formed a company to sell two or three pieces of candy wrapped in colossal quantities of paper stuffed into a gargantuan box. He would enter a store and draw a circle on a counter with his own anti-cockroach chalk. Next he extracted a pillbox from his pocket, opened it, and dropped two cockroaches into the middle of the circle. They fell over when they crossed the chalk line. Lewis always made the sale. After he left, the cockroaches came back to life, and the store owner realized the magic chalk had the power to stun the bugs, but not to kill.

University City City Hall

Lewis bought a magazine, the *Winner*, to sell his products, changed the name to the *Woman's Magazine* and dropped subscription prices to a dime. He soon claimed a circulation of a million and a half readers and was bringing in big revenue from advertising. He bought eighty-five acres in what would soon become University City and built such structures as the octagonal building on Delmar Boulevard for his publishing company. When the Louisiana Purchase Exposition came, he built a tent city with space for hundreds of penny-pinching visitors who paid a dollar a night.

Lewis then pitched a really big idea: a national bank with transactions done by mail, offering checking rather than postal money orders. It seemed a good way to overcome a dearth of banking services in many small towns. But postal inspectors decided that Lewis committed fraud by founding the People's United States Bank to raise money for his own enterprises. The post office returned all mail to the bank to senders, and the enterprise died. The post office also revoked the *Woman's Magazine*'s second-class mailing permit, which allowed the magazine to be mailed cheaply. Lewis was in serious trouble.

That didn't keep Lewis from thinking big. In 1906, he engineered the incorporation of an area west of St. Louis as University City. From 1906 to 1912, he was the first mayor of the city, which he correctly predicted would see outward growth from the exclusive Central West End. He bought a newspaper in 1908 and used it to boost his plan for subways. The scheme never materialized, and the old owners got it back in 1910 when he couldn't make the payments. The end was near. Three times he was acquitted of mail fraud charges, but by 1912 he was running out of money. The next year, he hightailed it out of town.

He stopped in California, halfway between Los Angeles and San Francisco, where he used five hundred dollars he raised as a down payment to buy twenty-three thousand acres and start a new town, called Atascadero. He founded a magazine and started selling lots. But he couldn't beat new postal fraud charges. Sentenced in 1928 to five years in prison, he was paroled in 1931 and told he'd be behind bars again if he started another of his businesses. Never mind that. He quickly started selling land and hawking another publication and was sent back behind bars until 1934.

In 1950, *St. Louis Globe-Democrat* writer Francis A. Klein reported Lewis's passing this way: "A fabulous personage, a blower of vast financial bubbles that cost the life savings of untold thousands of persons, died in obscurity and near-poverty the other day in Atascadero, Cal." Today, in University City and Atascadero, many remember him more kindly than Francis Klein did. People in both towns credit him for creating model cities. The octagonal building Lewis erected for his publishing interests is now University City City Hall. Atascadero has an E.G. Lewis Highway. Why not? A guy like that needs to know the best way out of town.

# Red Villa:
# Barkeep Alderman

With a stogie protruding from his mouth and a fedora atop his head, Eleventh Ward alderman Albert "Red" Villa was the picture of a Democratic big city pol in the middle of the twentieth century. When he wasn't at city hall, Villa received constituents at the Cottage, a working-class bar he ran. From 1953 until he died in 1990, he gained a reputation as a blunt and straight-shooting representative of those living at the far southern end of the city. "Always, my political base was the saloon," he said. "Politics is for saloonkeepers."

Villa's training for the job started early, when he was born in 1909, the son of immigrants from Milan, Italy. He attended St. Boniface Catholic School before he dropped out in the fourth grade to help make money for his family. He co-owned two taverns before he joined with James H. McAteer to buy the Cottage in 1931. Twice during Prohibition he was convicted of misdemeanor bootlegging violations. Villa watched as McAteer later was named clerk of the city circuit court of criminal causes. In 1951, Villa received an appointment to succeed McAteer. But there was a string attached: he had to sell the Cottage. He wasn't able to do that, and he quit the clerk position.

The working-class saloon attracted workers from such nearby industries as Coca-Cola, National Lead, and the Coast Guard. "It was rare to see a female in the tavern," said Red Villa's son, Thomas Villa, a former state representative and board of aldermen president who is the current Eleventh Ward alderman. After he was elected an alderman in 1953, Red Villa met with Eleventh Ward residents about issues ranging from potholes to jobs, at the saloon's Table No. 1. Thomas Villa recalls that his father banned jukeboxes from his watering hole. That prohibition lasted until Red Villa sold the bar in 1978. After a goodbye party that included Mayor James Conway and many other local pols, new owners Judy and Dave Reed introduced a jukebox and a Jukebox Saturday Night.

With or without a bar, Red Villa had a blunt way of expressing himself. He once refused to take a $2,500-a-year raise and chose instead to use the money for lights at baseball fields in Carondelet Park. Villa would have nothing to do with a push to attract more convention business by allowing topless dancers at big hotels. "You're not going to bring people to conventions here just so they can see eighteen girls dancing up and down without any tops on," he declared. He didn't buy the idea that a football stadium would pay for itself. "His famous line was 'Why the hell don't we build two stadiums? We're getting the first one for nothing,'" Thomas Villa said. "He was just very direct, and people got the message," said Red Villa's grandson, Matt Villa. The nephew of Thomas Villa, Matt Villa represented Red Villa's ward from 1998 to 2011.

Red Villa was direct to his last speech, given at the dedication of a bust made by local artist Bob Cassilly not long before his death from cancer in 1990. "My life in politics has been good. I have helped some people and had some fun," he said in a ceremony at a triangular park at Ivory and Virginia Avenues that is still home to the bust. In it, he is holding one of his stogies. Except for a two-day hiatus from office, Villa served longer than any other alderman since the adoption of a new city charter in 1914. That break came when he was the target of a 1967 suit by the circuit attorney's office because he lived outside the ward at 3841 Holly Hills Boulevard. He resigned from the board and moved to 510 Dover Place in the Eleventh Ward. The board of aldermen quickly voted to reinstate Villa. He put a sign in front of the house that said "Red Villa Lives Here." Before he died, the aldermanic chambers where he had sat for thirty-seven years were renamed after him. At the foot of his desk was a brass spittoon.

# James Eagan: The Green Man of Florissant

As Irish as a four-leaf clover, James J. Eagan coated the wallpaper, the lampshades, and the paneling on his desk at Florissant City Hall with bright green. When he arrived at work in his green Mercury, he got to the bottom of things by plopping into a green chair in his office. Possessed of wavy, whiter-than-white hair and a green tie, this man known as the "Jolly Green Giant" held forth for thirty-seven years as mayor of the largest city in St. Louis County. A letter from him came signed in green ink. But when he decided to coat a city-owned World War II era tank with Kelly green paint, veterans decided he'd crossed the green line. "In my opinion, if he had his way, he'd paint the tombstones in the cemetery Kelly green," squawked a vet who led the charge against the paint job. The Irish in him may have helped account for the quotes he lavished on newshawks and the rhubarbs he always seemed to whip up. He loved God, he loved his family, and he loved Florissant.

He was born thirteen days before St. Patrick's Day in 1926 and grew up in a strongly Democratic Irish Catholic area of North St. Louis. He graduated from McBride High School on North Kingshighway Boulevard and spent World War II in the navy in the Pacific. A graduate of St. Louis University School of Law, he moved to the Florissant area in 1949 when it was still rural. Florissant only had around 3,800 citizens in 1950 but exploded to more than 70,000 a quarter century later. He settled down, raised a family, and started getting involved in the rapidly growing community.

He was elected to the Woodson Terrace Board of Trustees in 1953 but lost a bid for mayor of that community the following year. In 1958, he was elected a magistrate for the Florissant area. Five years later, after helping to lead a successful effort to replace Florissant's 107-year-old charter, he ran for mayor against the incumbent mayor,

Henry F. Koch. Koch opposed the charter and had the support of union steamfitters. Eagan's good-government campaign called for ridding the streets of motorists who regularly violated traffic laws, rescinding the annexation of 5,400 nearby acres forced through under the old charter, enforcing ordinances without favoritism, and keeping city offices open one night a week. Voters swept in Eagan and other charter supporters, heralding a new day for Florissant. He never lost a race for mayor after that.

Eagan quickly took steps to ensure the city's affairs were done in a "businesslike" manner. "Our police don't fix tickets, and they give no balls to raise money. We have competent people, send them to school, and pay them professional salaries," he said. But some said he went too far when he monitored calls to city hall to ensure employees responded politely or when he put the kibosh on plays planned for the civic center. Calls flooded his office when *The Boys in the Band*, a play about a group of gay men, was performed at the civic center. After that, he approved the plays first. "We don't like his censorship," Mrs. Richard Selle, a board member of the Hawthorne Players, one group that performed at the civic center, said in 1974. "I think he just puts on a show for the little old ladies of Florissant."

Eagan irked fellow Democrats when he endorsed John Cooper, the Republican mayor of Webster Groves in 1972, for the congressional seat then held by a Democrat, James W. Symington. In spite of this show of independence, he ran an unsuccessful race in 1974 for the Democratic nomination for St. Louis County supervisor, an office akin to county executive now. He thought about running for the Democratic nomination for governor in 1976 but decided against it. Two years later, he snatched the Democratic nomination for county executive but lost to Republican Gene McNary.

From then on, his attention was on serving his constituents in Florissant. In 1999, running again for reelection, he pointed to $48 million in new commercial development in the city in the previous four years as evidence that all still was golden in Florissant. His opponent, former city councilman David Reynolds, said that Eagan had been a great mayor but noted uneasily that property values were flat and people were leaving town.

Nonetheless, Eagan defeated Reynolds in his tenth consecutive run for mayor, as he had beaten all the other challenges. But there was one fight he had to lose. Before he could run again, he died at seventy-four in 2000. "He did politics and governance at the retail level, sitting down at card tables in grocery stores, stopping at traffic lights and jumping out of his green Mercury," the *Post-Dispatch* editorialized. "Approachable? No. He approached you."

# Bill Bangert: The World's Strongest Mayor

Read the story of Bill Bangert's life, and you'll wonder whether it's actually the tales of four or five memorable human beings mushed into one. A star in several sports in high school and college and an Olympic prospect, he signed as a professional football player and grabbed track and field awards in his seventies. Standing six feet five inches and weighing 265 pounds, he was a prospective opera singer, a city mayor, and part-owner of a family road-building company. He was blinded but regained sight in one eye with experimental surgery. But the wildest part of his story was a scheme to create a mighty sports complex in northwestern St. Louis County. The complex wasn't built, but he talked about it until he died in 2011 at the age of eighty-seven.

Bangert grew up in Berkeley and starred in baseball, football, and boxing in high school. He excelled in football, shot put, and discus at the University of Missouri and later at Purdue University. He won the National AAU discus championships in 1944 and 1945, was a three-time National AAU shot put champion, and successfully auditioned with the Metropolitan Opera. Back in St. Louis, he met, wooed, and wed a former Muny Opera singer while both were soloists at Central Presbyterian Church in Clayton. He entered the road construction business with his two brothers and was elected mayor of Berkeley in 1950.

Bangert's future seemed bright until blood vessels behind the retinas of both of his eyes hemorrhaged, blinding him at the age of twenty-eight. But he refused to put his life on pause. He wanted to get into the Olympics in 1952 and offered to give a benefit concert for the Olympic Fund. After being led to the shot put rink at the National AAU championships, he placed fourth. Three months later, he saw his sixteen-month-old daughter after undergoing successful experimental surgery to bring back sight in his right

eye. The sight never returned to his left eye. Then he ran as a
Republican for Congress. Soon after that, while driving through
Berkeley at midnight, a bullet struck his car. It may have been a
stray bullet, or it may have been a warning from a political enemy;
Bangert never knew. But splinters from broken glass struck his
still-blind left eye.

Bangert resigned as Berkeley mayor in 1957 after residents
voted to eliminate his position in favor of a council-manager
government. The next year, he quit the family road-building
company to focus his attention on an idea as big as himself. Near
what would become the southwest corner of Interstates 70 and
270, he hoped to erect a 100,000-seat domed stadium big enough
to lure the Pan American Games and the 1964 Summer Olympics.
Bangert planned a racetrack, bomb shelters for hundreds of
thousands, convention space, a monumental restaurant in the
stadium's roof, monorails, and one of the biggest malls anywhere.
He arranged for the incorporation of the village of Champ, where
the super-development would be, and became its mayor. He
promoted a financing scheme not that different from today's tax
increment financing, with business and industry leases and the
sale of $87.5 million in bonds paying for the deal. It seemed the
dream might come true when the Missouri legislature approved
the bonds, but Governor James Blair ended everything with a
veto. It didn't help that business interests promoting the proposed
downtown Busch Stadium opposed him. Within years, Bangert
went bankrupt and lost property and his home in the town. The
town now has about fourteen inhabitants and a quarry.

Bangert kept planning something big in Champ, but he finally
gave up and moved to California, where he managed commercial
properties and sang with his wife in Christian operas and in the
choir of televangelist Robert Schuller's *Hour of Power*. Eventually, he
moved back and lived in a home in Marthasville. He floated the idea
of a new two-hundred-acre island at the confluence of the Mississippi
and Missouri Rivers with a fountain shooting a thousand feet in

the air. Bangert still exercised with all his might, competed where he could, spent time examining the *more than three dozen medals* on his wall that he won after his seventieth birthday, and reminisced about days gone by. One memory was about how he won a gallon of malt whiskey in Scotland in 1971 for receiving the title of "World's Strongest Mayor." He was a big man in every way and would have maintained a titanic presence even if he hadn't weighed 265 pounds and stood six feet five inches.

# Dakin Williams:
# In His Brother's Shadow

Walter Dakin Williams always thought of himself as a "professional brother." Dakin's sibling, famous playwright Tennessee Williams, called Dakin "my improbable little brother." So it's no surprise that this sibling of Tennessee Williams would want to portray characters in his brother's plays. But when Dakin dressed in drag to perform the part of Blanche DuBois in his brother's play *A Streetcar Named Desire*, a New York television critic said enough was enough. Budd Schulberg contended that Dakin's 1988 portrayal in New York of the tragic heroine was "a travesty of great American literature." It didn't stop the Collinsville attorney from reprising the performance that year in Key West, Florida, and at the New Orleans Tennessee Williams/New Orleans Literary Festival. It was one of the ways he sought to take attention off his more famous brother.

Dakin Williams's resume would be impressive, even if he hadn't been the brother of one of the best American playwrights of the twentieth century. He graduated from University City High School and received his joint bachelor of arts–law degree from Washington University in 1942. He spent six months at the Harvard University Graduate School of Business before being drafted into the army during World War II. He was called back for service in the 1950s and served as a military defense and prosecuting attorney. After that, he was an assistant US attorney and then a private attorney in Collinsville. Residents of the east side of the Mississippi knew him for his collections of Oriental carvings and furniture, as a chef and gourmet, and for the books he self-published.

But the fame of Tennessee Williams pushed him to run again and again for governor and senator in the 1970s and 1980s. Running against incumbent senator Adlai Stevenson III in 1974, the *Wall Street Journal* reported, "he distributed to the press a coyly posed nude photograph of himself and challenged Mr. Stevenson to follow a similar disclosure policy. 'It illustrates the fact that I have nothing to hide.'" In that same campaign, Williams performed a most odd exorcism of corruption in the biggest city in Illinois. Using a New Testament story that told how Jesus cast demons from a possessed man into a throng of pigs, Williams showed up at Chicago City Hall and asked someone to hold a "Herd of Swine" sign. He then transferred the "evil spirits" from politicians like Mayor Richard J. Daley to the "pigs." The stunt got him time on the 6 p.m. and 10 p.m. news on all the Chicago television stations. Reporters and TV crews flocked to one of Dakin's events when his apolitical brother showed up and said he admired Dakin's "guts" and honesty for running.

Tennessee might have come to one of Dakin's campaign gatherings, but relations between the two weren't particularly warm. Tennessee was angry that Dakin brought him from New York to Barnes-Jewish Hospital in St. Louis in 1969 for several months of hospitalization for drug and alcohol abuse. The intervention saved Tennessee's life, but he didn't see it that way. After that, relations between the two were cold. After Tennessee died in 1983, his will cut Dakin out of nearly a $10 million fortune. Of that, Dakin was to receive just $25,000, but only after the death of his sister Rose.

For his part, Dakin reportedly ignored Tennessee's desire that his body be buried at sea north of Cuba and arranged for his brother to be buried next to his mother in the family plot in Calvary Cemetery in St. Louis. "Tennessee is such a literary personality that his grave should be where people can visit it," Dakin said at the time. Later, Dakin told the *Riverfront Times* that two co-trustees of Tennessee's estate, not he, had made the decision to bury and not cremate him. After that, he decided to have him buried in St. Louis rather than in the home of his maternal grandparents in Waynesville, Ohio.

Dakin kept writing books about his brother, including one that claimed the playwright was murdered. Authorities said Tennessee choked to death on February 25, 1983, on a plastic cap similar to the one used for eye or nose drops. Dakin claimed a female friend of Tennessee was responsible. And he often appeared and performed his own offbeat interpretation of his brother's plays at the Tennessee Williams/New Orleans Literary Festival. At such events, he had to deal with those who claimed he was there to capitalize on his brother's fame. When he died at the age of eighty-nine in 2008, Dakin Williams was buried next to his brother, his mother, and Rose. In life, Tennessee Williams overshadowed his brother. But in death, they found equality in the same family burial plot.

# Mickey McTague:
# Master of the Laugh Line

Mickey McTague's grandfather kept customers of his downtown restaurant happy with the best seafood in town and the latest scuttlebutt about everything. Mickey's father was a St. Louis pol with an eye on a higher office. It's no surprise, then, that people knew Mickey as a writer of jokes for comedians and a friend of politicians and reporters from the 1960s until he died in 2011. Mickey was always ready with

firsthand stories of the entertainers and local muckety-mucks he knew as friends. Mickey put it best when he said, "I have known big men in the government house, and I have known government men in the big house."

The stories Mickey told always included how his grandfather James Hugh McTague started a restaurant in the Century Building downtown before the start of the twentieth century. Its reputation grew mightily, as William Marion Reedy's *Mirror* reported in 1911. "Lobsters, oysters, crabs, clams, all the rarer and choicer kinds of fish—these are to be had at McTague's exactly as they may be had at the seashore," the magazine said. "Then there's McTague himself—he's always on deck looking after things and he's good to talk to, whether on theology, baseball, or politics."

Mickey's father, Marshall McTague Sr., took a different path. He was the city condemnation commissioner and Seventh Ward Democratic committeeman and was being eyed for a run for governor. Mickey—whose name was actually Marshall Jr.—was nine when he went with his father to a rally for President Harry Truman. Mickey got a handshake from Truman and remembered the president holding up his *Post-Dispatch* with scorn because the paper didn't endorse him. When the senior McTague died suddenly right after Mickey's eighth-grade graduation, Mickey was stunned and became a leader of sorts for his family. But it didn't keep him from making people laugh.

Hearing that a comedian named Jerry Lester would perform at a local hotel, he went there and handed Lester a script he'd written. Lester used some of what Mickey made up. In 1959, Mickey bought an airplane ticket to Cleveland, where Bob Hope was set to entertain. There, he contrived a meeting with Hope and showed him a script. Hope recognized Mickey from a brief conversation he'd had with him earlier in St. Louis and looked at the piece. The comedian loved it and agreed to use it. It led to a long working relationship with Hope, especially when Hope came to St. Louis and needed locally oriented jokes.

Soon Mickey was writing jokes for such entertainers as Lenny Bruce and Joe Garagiola. From his typewriter came jokes like this: "I know a guy who had such bad luck that he lost fifty dollars trying to hit the jackpot on a stamp machine." And this: "[The Gateway Arch] cost $26 million. One million dollars for the stainless steel and mortar and $25 million to bend it." In the late sixties, he talked of writing comedy for a living and relocating. But when American Greeting Cards asked him whether he wanted to work for that company at its headquarters in Cleveland, he wrote this zinger to turn the offer down: "Cannot relocate now, and that would be a hell of a drive every morning from St. Louis to West

78th Street in Cleveland." He still thought of moving to the West Coast to work in comedy but stayed here and toiled for the city.

He spent most of his career as a patronage worker for St. Louis before he retired in 2007. He lost bids for city offices three times, worked for such mayors as Raymond Tucker and A. J. Cervantes, and hung out with the likes of Senator Thomas Eagleton and Governor Mel Carnahan. He developed a reputation for knowing everybody and sometimes did things that might come out of a movie script he would have written in Hollywood. As related by *Post-Dispatch* columnist Bill McClellan, Mickey dropped into Kelly's Korner saloon downtown around Christmastime, just before he planned to deliver legal papers for the sheriff's department. As he drank with the bar's owner, he discovered he was getting ready to hand out a pile of eviction notices and garnishments during a season meant for joy. Mickey threw the papers away, to the cheers of the tavern's customers. Mickey also showed he still could write comedy after McClellan accepted an invitation to do a commencement speech for St. Louis University at the last minute. Mickey helpfully banged out an oration for the columnist. One line was, "Just remember, if you don't succeed, you have something in common with your commencement speaker." McClellan included that part, but not the rest of the speech. Whether his audience was a columnist, a politician, or a whole audience, Mickey McTague knew how to make them laugh.

# Bill Haas: Don Quixote in St. Louis

L ate in 1996, Bill Haas took time out from his campaign for St. Louis mayor to make a request. He ran personal ads seeking an independently wealthy wife to finance his campaigns. Haas, who lost that election, claims he did it to show that he shouldn't have to raise trucks full of cash to be a viable candidate. Had the ads gotten him a spouse with deep pockets, she would have paid a lot to underwrite his growing list of campaigns for everything from mayor to state representative to alderman to Congress. Haas's ads, his unusual quotes, and his continual runs for office have made him good copy for local reporters for nearly a quarter of a century.

A Cleveland native, Haas worked as a corporate lawyer and got involved in politics in his hometown after he graduated from Yale and Harvard Law School. He worked in the successful campaign of Dennis Kucinich for Cleveland mayor in 1977 and made losing runs for that city's school board in 1981 and city council in 1988. Later in 1988, he took a corporate law job in St. Louis. Laid off in 1991 when his corporation went into bankruptcy, he's worked since then in such jobs as a customer service manager at Walmart, an adjunct professor, and a high school math teacher. In 1992,

acting on his desire to seek public office, he ran for St. Louis circuit attorney.

More campaigns followed, and local voters soon found he was talking about more than issues. "William C. Haas's campaign is a mix of oddities and serious dissertations on issues," said a *Post-Dispatch* profile during the 1997 mayoral race. The profile noted that a campaign brochure included a picture of Haas with two dogs identified as his campaign staff. "Serious stuff gets boring if you don't lighten it up. The picture might win me the animal vote," Haas said then. Haas lost the 1993 and 1997 mayoral races but won a seat on the St. Louis School Board in 1997.

He soon was in trouble for strong language in messages left on the KMOX comment line for talk show host Charlie Brennan. "How can I say this nicely. . . . Do the words 'Kiss my ass' mean anything to you?" he said. The school board promised to investigate, and Brennan said Haas's words were the ramblings of a man trying to make a point through grade-school humor. "He may not know that teachers are fired for using such language," said school board president Marybeth McBryan. Haas apologized for the comments, made after Brennan criticized him. To show that there were no hard feelings, Brennan wrote a front cover blurb to Haas's 2015 self-published novel, *Pink Collar Blue*.

Haas kept making news. He got the school board to approve a policy prohibiting harassment and discrimination against LGBT students and staff. At his urging, the city health department agreed to make contraceptives available to students. And he kept running for office. A 2001 *Post-Dispatch* profile about yet another run for mayor that year, titled "Haas Draws Laughs, but Insists Candidacy Is No Joke," included the detail that Haas frequently left reporters voice mails up to twenty minutes long after midnight.

People didn't laugh in 2005 when Haas wrote in a blog that he'd thought of suicide because of his deteriorating financial situation. Haas said in 2015 that he had dealt with depression since the mid-1960s and pointed out the blog to a reporter so he might know how to write about it if he did commit suicide. He contends that he was surprised the post made headlines. In his defense, Haas said, "I think the same part of me that has made me fragile when life seems so difficult to endure is the same part of me that fights so hard for the welfare of others."

It may seem that Haas is tilting at windmills, but it's wrong to say he never won. He was elected four times to the St. Louis School Board and won the 2008 Democratic nomination for the US representative seat held by conservative Republican Todd Akin. But Akin beat Haas in the general election, and the school board lost most of its power when a state-controlled board took over the city's public schools in 2007 after they lost their accreditation. After losing the August 2016 primary race against Democratic First District US Representative Lacy Clay, he'd lost a total of seventeen races, including the two in Cleveland. But Haas still dreams voters someday will elect him to a major office. Said Haas: "I'm going to keep chasing those dreams as long as I am able."

# MAVERICKS & RENEGADES

# Beatle Bob: He Never Stops Dancing

One day twenty years ago, Bob Matonis went to a rock concert. He went to another one the next night, another the night after that, and still another the night after that. On February 24, 2016, he claims, he spent his seven thousandth night in a row away from home and at a live music show. Even if he's missed a few nights, it seems the man better known as Beatle Bob never stops. "As long as there's good bands out there, local or national, I'll keep it going," he said. Matonis maintains a Beatles mop-top on his head, in honor of his all-time favorite foursome. His nickname came from a nun in the sixth grade at Mount Providence School for Boys in Florissant. Inside the geography book he'd been assigned to read was a copy of *16* magazine devoted entirely to the Beatles. "She raced down the aisle and snatched the magazine out of my hand," Matonis said. "'That'll be enough of that, Beatle Bob.'" The name stuck.

Everything was right for Matonis to soak up the rock culture of the 1960s, especially the British Invasion. The music was ubiquitous in elementary school, as he spent Mondays through Fridays at Mount Providence and weekends shuffling between his divorced parents in South St. Louis and his mother's parents in the

Baden area. Neighbors held rock 'n' roll parties in their backyards. The sounds of KXOK, the reigning rock station in town, always blared from his mother's radio. That continued as he attended Augustinian Academy and graduated from Southwest High School in 1971. "You had drive-ins where some of the bands would play before the movie," he said.

Matonis saw a change after he got his bachelor's degree in social work from the University of Missouri–St. Louis in 1975. The club scene started growing in the late 1970s and then really grew in the early 1980s. He went out a lot, but it turned into an obsession in the 1990s. The obsession moved to a new level on Christmas Day 1996, when Beatle Bob started regularly visiting the hottest act of the night. Since then, he's developed a reputation for turning a merely cool night of music into a memorable time just above absolute zero. He's been on KDHX and writes for the local website onstl.com. He hosts festivals and introduces bands on stage. In 2006, he received an all-expenses-paid trip to Puerto Penasco, Mexico, to host the Circus Mexicus Festival.

It's not always easy keeping that streak up, especially since Matonis doesn't drive. He gets rides from friends, workers at clubs—anyone he can find. That doesn't stop him. "It's the overall club experience," he said one night early in 2016, as he ate a veggie burger and a salad at the Blueberry Hill diner in the Delmar Loop. A vegetarian lifestyle helps give him the strength to keep going, he said, as do long and frequent bike rides and a refusal to smoke, drink, or take drugs.

He needed that strength one night early in 2016, when he made his presence known at a concert in Blueberry Hill's basement, the Duck Room. That night early in 2016, he introduced singer and steel guitar player Roger Clyne, who pumped the crowd for more than an hour with stories and songs from his latest album. Throughout the concert, Beatle Bob gyrated back and forth near the side of the stage. "If you see him at a show, it's supposed to be the best show of the night," said John Friss, who represented the promoter on the night of the Blueberry Hill concert. "If he meets you, he will remember your name and anything you tell him for the rest of your life. He must have a photographic memory," Friss said. "He's a good presenter at the beginning of it, and it's very entertaining to see him off to the side dancing."

Ron Stevens, a longtime local radio personality and webmaster for onstl.com, said Matonis displays a passion for music in a town that loves music. "It's very difficult to go out and appreciate live music without encountering Beatle Bob." Stevens first heard of Matonis after he and his wife moved back to St. Louis after spending time in Los Angeles, New York, and San Diego. After the two met about ten years ago, Matonis started writing a blog for onstl.com. "I believe he crashed a party at our house," Stevens said, recalling their first meeting. "When Beatle Bob crashes a party, it's a compliment."

# John Smith T: The Gentleman Duelist

Something Colonel John Smith T said about Lionel Browne's sister stuck in Browne's craw and wouldn't dislodge. So he challenged Smith to a duel, and they met near the Mississippi River in Monroe County, Illinois, to settle the matter. Both were handed cocked pistols and told they could fire after the count of "one" but not after "three." Just as a referee started to say the word "one," a ball from Smith's gun pierced Browne's forehead. Browne was dead on the ground by the count of three.

Browne should have known better. In the years after the start of the nineteenth century, folks in southeast Missouri knew that a challenge to duel John Smith T came with a death wish. Many stories exist of a man with more than his share of the male hormone shooting one, two, or three opponents in duels. But few had Smith's record. John F. Darby, who was St. Louis's mayor from 1835 to 1837 and 1840 to 1841, noted in his memoirs reports that Smith claimed he had killed fifteen men, mostly in duels. Originally from Georgia, he moved to Tennessee and changed his name to "Smith T" (for Tennessee) to distinguish himself from all the other John Smiths. He moved again to Ste. Genevieve County, Missouri, and became a judge of the Ste. Genevieve Court of Common Pleas.

Wherever Smith traveled, his instruments of death were by his side. Under his coat were two pistols on a belt. Usually, he had two pocket pistols in a coat pocket and a long dagger next to his breast. A slave spent all his time in a gunsmith shop keeping Smith's guns, pistols, and rifles in the perfect shape for the kill. Many ran when they saw Smith coming. Others needed convincing. An old militia general once approached Smith while he was drinking wine on a Sunday afternoon at the City Hotel in St. Louis. The man uttered a sentence that Smith took as a slur. Smith removed his pistol from his belt and placed it by his plate. Seeing this, the old general quickly left the dining room and made sure he stayed away from Smith.

Darby wasn't among those who feared Smith. "A man of more polished manners and more courteous demeanor I never met. He was a gentleman in every respect. John Smith T killed most of the men he shot in fair and open duels, where his own life was at stake; in what, in his day and time, was considered honorable, open, manly warfare," wrote Darby, a lawyer who occasionally did business with Smith. "And when he killed any man in any sudden quarrel or broil, he always stood his trial, and was always honorably acquitted by a jury of his country. He was as polished and courteous a gentleman as ever lived in the state of Missouri, and 'as mild a mannered man as ever put a bullet into the human body.'"

Otho Schrader, the coroner around Ste. Genevieve, learned an odd lesson about Smith's kindness. He came to Smith's home to arrest him for treason for his involvement in a plot against the government by Aaron Burr, who had been vice president under Thomas Jefferson. In that plot, Burr sought to split the western United States from the eastern United States. But as Schrader rode up to Smith's home around suppertime one night, Smith had a different idea. "I know what you have come for: you have come with a writ to arrest me. If you attempt it, you are a dead man. I will not be arrested," Smith announced. "It is a great outrage to indict me for treason. I'm as good a friend to the United States as any man in this territory." Then Smith added, "Mr. Schrader, dinner is just ready—get down and come in and take dinner; but mark, if you attempt to move a finger, or make a motion to arrest me, you are a dead man." Smith arranged to have Schrader sit across from him, so his guest could see a cocked and loaded pistol next to his host's plate. Ever the good host, Smith kept asking if Schrader liked his soup or would take more. Schrader rode off with the memory of a delicious meal, and nobody ever arrested Smith for the infraction.

# Tony Faust:
# A Taste of Heaven

For the rich and the famous in St. Louis at the end of the nineteenth century, no meal was worth eating if it didn't come from the kitchen of Tony Faust's Oyster House and Restaurant. Near the swank Southern Hotel and the Olympic Theatre, the city's beau monde congregated with visitors from afar and great actors after a performance to feast on the best oysters, lobsters, steak, and beer west of Chicago. The regulars included beer baron Adolphus Busch. He was known for winning one hundred dollar bets on whether he could identify any kind of

wine poured into a glass. Another patron once won a bet by eating 256 oysters from the half shell at one sitting. He finished his evening with a porterhouse steak, potatoes au gratin, and a stein of beer. Faust's Restaurant was a regular stopping place for the city's rich and famous.

The author of those feasts—Tony Faust—was born in Prussia in 1835 and came to the United States in 1853. He found work as an ornamental plasterer but went into the restaurant business because of a military accident at the start of the Civil War. It happened on May 10, 1861, the day St. Louis Germans provided the men to take over the secessionist-leaning state militia gathering at the edge of St. Louis called Camp Jackson. As Faust watched those soldiers, one stumbled and accidentally fired his gun. Faust took a bullet in

his side that weakened him enough that
he no longer could plaster. He looked
around for another way to make a living
and decided to start a bar at Broadway
and Russell Avenue. He established
Faust's in 1868.

The restaurant at Broadway and
Elm Street was so progressive that
Faust started lighting the inside of
his building with electricity in 1878,
eleven years before the city's streets.
Its offerings included Faust Beer,
brewed by Anheuser-Busch and
named in honor of Tony Faust. Faust
did so well with his restaurant that
he established Faust's Fulton Market,

Oyster Depot, and Packing House to sell such products as oysters,
sea fish, lobsters, crabs, and clams. He sold cheeses from England,
Germany, France, and Switzerland, as well as game in season.
So his customers could have the best product possible, he had a
schooner built in the Chesapeake Bay.

Meanwhile, Faust's relationship with Anheuser-Busch kept
growing. When the brewery introduced its new super-premium
Michelob beer in 1896, Faust's was the first to serve it. Family
connections helped. Besides managing the family restaurant and
being vice president of the Fourth National Bank of St. Louis,
Faust's son Edward was second vice president of Anheuser-Busch
Brewing Co. Adolphus Busch married off his fourth daughter,
Anna Louise Busch, to Eddie Faust on March 20, 1897.

While this went on, Faust and August Lüchow partnered in a
colossal restaurant at the 1904 St. Louis World's Fair. Supposedly
the biggest eatery in the world, the Luchow-Faust Restaurant had
inside and outside seating for 7,500 customers. Oodles of such
business dealings put Faust at the top of the city's elite when he

died in 1906. After his death, the restaurant was managed by his son Anthony E. Faust Jr., before it passed through two other owners and shut down in 1916.

The great restaurant was just a memory, but members of Faust's family kept doing notable things for the St. Louis area. A 197-acre tract in present-day Chesterfield donated to St. Louis County in 1968 by Tony Faust's grandson Leicester Faust and his wife, Mary Plant Faust, became Faust Park. And in 2015, Anheuser-Busch resurrected the recipe for Faust Beer and began selling it again in draft beer in such select St. Louis locations as the Biergarten and Budweiser Brew House at Ballpark Village in downtown St. Louis. A toast raised with the Vienna-style lager is enough to bring back stories of how Tony Faust treated his customers right.

There was, for example, a man named Joseph Jefferson who arrived for supper one night at midnight. "Bring me quail on sauerkraut," he demanded. It wasn't on the menu, but the chefs obliged. "Magnificent," he said. Others agreed, and it soon was a favorite at Faust's. A Harvard University historian named John Fiske wrote of one especially sumptuous meal he and two others had in Faust's dining room in 1887. They feasted on oxtail soup, cucumbers, sweet potatoes, chateaubriand aux champignons (beef with mushrooms), and asparagus on toast. They finished the meal with strawberries and ice cream, Roquefort cheese, and cafe noir. On New Year's Eve, Faust sat with his wife and family at a table in the center of the main dining room. At midnight, waiters placed bottles of wine in front of every patron, "with the compliments of Mr. Faust."

# Tom Goabout: Champion of the Poultry Pilferers

Baseball has its world champion, hockey its Stanley Cup, and soccer its World Cup. Tom Goabout was a champion in his own class, so much so that the *Post-Dispatch* made mention of him at least seventy times from 1885 to 1903. It was a championship most would not seek but that Tom Goabout would love. For he was a champion of stealing chickens and swiping dogs. Once police caught up with him after he'd stuffed two hens into a gunny sack in one yard and then jumped a fence to another yard, where he placed two ducks into another sack. The cops nabbed him and used the birds for evidence. "What kind of chickens do you steal, Tom?" a *Post-Dispatch* article quoted an interrogator in 1885. "Only fightin' chickens. I don' take no eatin' chickens. I got no use for 'em," the paper said.

Over the years, the *Post-Dispatch* devoted deep vats full of ink to Goabout's various incarcerations in the city jail, the city workhouse, and state penitentiaries. But he always made his way out again to terrorize chickens, dogs, and owners of both. Tom Goabout made good copy. There were those who said Goabout had hypnotic power over dogs he pursued to purloin. "It is his boast that he can enter a strange yard or house on the darkest night and make away with the fiercest bulldog . . . or any breed of dog without arousing the suspicions of the owner and without permitting the animal to make the slightest noise or resistance," the paper said.

The life of a stealer of dogs and chickens wasn't easy. In 1894, he showed up in the city dispensary, badly beaten. He told a doctor that white men had set upon him after he cast eyes on a white woman. But police concluded that Goabout's brother Lewis Goabout had administered the beating because the notorious animal thief was being too friendly with his girlfriend. A police officer shot Goabout in 1897, and a man wielding a large beer glass beat him and cut him in the face in 1900. Two brothers, including Lewis, died of gunshot wounds after the start of the twentieth century. In 1903, the *Post-Dispatch* noted that Tom Goabout was serving time in a penitentiary for killing an unidentified member of his family. Whatever happened to Tom Goabout after that isn't certain, but one can presume that the dogs and chickens of St. Louis rested easier with him behind bars.

# Will Greensburg:
# A Newsie Makes It Big

illie Greenburg was the image of one who pulls himself up by the bootstraps, all with his earnings from selling papers. Years after he died, the *Post-Dispatch* said of him that his career "served as a life illustration of young men to get ahead." A real-life Horatio Alger, he became the newsboy for mayors, bankers, and industrialists and the possessor of a fortune garnered from investing his receipts in real estate. When he died in 1911 at the age of thirty-three, a front-page headline in the *St. Louis Republic* called him the Richest Newsboy in St. Louis. It described Willie Greenburg, but it didn't say everything. The whole truth was that he was a rare escapee from a life that destroyed too many boys.

Willie Greenburg entered the tough world of the newsie around the age of ten, about five years after he arrived with his parents in America from Germany. It was around 1890 when he

started hawking papers on Olive Street. His brother Ben sold with him and often took time off to fight the bullies who wanted Will's spot. After Willie was rich, the *Post-Dispatch* said this of those early days: "It seems not so very long ago that he was a little dark-haired, black-eyed 'kid' dodging wagons and hopping cars in the downtown district and advertising his wares with a shrill tremelo cry 'paper here.'"

An old photograph makes newsies look tough, puffing smoke from cigarettes, newsboy's caps atop their heads. But in the last decade of the nineteenth century, the life of a newsboy was full of misery. Many were orphans who might be beaten if they didn't sell their quota of newspapers. Robbers might deprive them of their receipts. After they sold papers at bars and brothels, they might spend their earnings at the same places. Dirty and pitiful, most had a bleak future.

In this world, the Greenburg brothers sold hard, and after ten years Ben and Willie had saved enough pennies to buy a diminutive stand outside the Merchants-Laclede Building at Fourth and Olive Streets. The stand in the middle of the city's financial district may have been small, but it was the perfect place for him to rub shoulders with the city's potentates of finance. David R. Francis, the former mayor and governor who got St. Louis the Louisiana Purchase Exposition, and Rolla Wells, the mayor from 1901 to 1909, were among those who stopped by the stand. Willie coaxed more coins out of his customers' deep pockets by adding magazines to his selection. Bankers and brokers who stayed around the stand to gossip gave Willie tips on the best investments. Willie kept the advice in mind for the right time.

"O, Willie is the candy kid, all right," Ben told the *Post-Dispatch* in 1909. "He's got the money, and he deserves it. He always was a bear for work." The article told how Willie and Ben moved out of the cold into the lobby of the Merchants-Laclede Building. And it told how Willie spent $112,000 in 1909—that's $2.7 million in 2015 money—to build the Knickerbocker Apartments at Taylor and McPherson Avenues. The cash rolled in, as lawyers, doctors, and businessmen paid rents of six hundred to nine hundred dollars for the privilege of living at that exclusive Central West End address. Willie didn't think much of the praise he received for his accomplishments. "What is so wonderful about a fellow working hard and saving his money?" he asked.

The *St. Louis Republic* apparently thought a lot of such a fellow. The paper showered him with prizes ranging from horses and buggies to gold watches for selling the most papers. Bankers often sent him letters praising him for rising from poverty. It was splendid, but it wasn't enough to spare him a fate that might befall one of the poorly clad orphan newsies out in the frigid street. At thirty-three, the rich bachelor fell ill with pneumonia. He died five days later.

At the end of 1911, the *Post-Dispatch* reported that Ben had bought a license to marry an aspiring opera singer named Sophia Golland. The article was in the style papers used for the marriages of the rich, complete with a photo of the bride in a flowing gown. And why shouldn't Ben be rich? After all, Willie had left the Knickerbocker Apartments and his newsstand to him. But Ben's life as the new richest newsboy in St. Louis wasn't to last. He died in June 1917 at the Knickerbocker Apartments, a victim of pneumonia. Once a newsie, always a newsie.

# Robert "Hot Rod" Moore: Flooring It on Portland Place

R obert H. Moore's slicked-back hair made him look like James Dean in *Rebel Without a Cause*. He certainly played the part of a rebel. He was the perfect character for a 1950s record about a speed demon who always eludes the police. For much of the early fifties, St. Louis papers were stuffed with stories about how he raced down city and county streets, avoiding pursuing police cruisers, slamming into cars, and exasperating lawmen who tried to keep him off the streets. He was eighteen when police cited him the first time and made news for his speeding tickets into the early 1960s, after he turned thirty. In 1998 the *Post-Dispatch* stated that he received twenty-four or twenty-eight citations altogether—the exact number isn't certain. Headline writers called him "Hot Rod Moore."

The son of a prosperous doctor who lived on moneyed Portland Place, Moore was first arrested for going through a stop sign on December 5, 1948. He ran up five more tickets before August 1949, when city police cracked down on him for racing around the track on Sherman Park near Cote Brilliante Avenue. Moore stopped only when police fired a shot. His driving privileges were revoked in St. Louis but not in the state. Police arrested him again in May 1950 after he was clocked at eighty miles per hour racing a buddy on Lindbergh Boulevard. Moore's father, Dr. Harry H. Moore, promised to let his son stay in jail for the infraction. But the Automobile Club of Missouri put up three hundred dollars for bail, and Hot Rod Moore went free. Prosecutors thought they had a good case against him, but witnesses against him either wouldn't testify or vanished. Those infractions were just part of the long list of Hot Rod Moore's violations. To keep out of jail, he tried to enlist in the military. The armed services turned his application down, saying they weren't running a correctional institution. When Hot Rod's father took his car away, his mother gave him another one.

Editorial writers demanded action. "The picture of frustrated police and frustrated courts which this record presents is hardly calculated to serve a young man as the best guide to his future conduct," the *Post-Dispatch* said. The *Globe-Democrat* was sterner. "How long are Robert H. Moore, teen-age hot-rod driver, and his attorney going to be permitted to make a mockery of law enforcement in the St. Louis Courts?" it asked. Republican candidate Robert Neumann told voters he would put Moore behind bars if he was elected St. Louis County circuit attorney. In August 1953, just a few months after he was elected, Mayor Raymond R. Tucker heard an appeal from the president of the Boys Town of Missouri to "find a way" to stop Moore from continuing his mischief.

Justice seemed to come near the end of the summer of 1954, when Moore pleaded guilty in Audrain County Circuit Court to one count of leaving the scene of damage to property, a felony. St. Louis circuit attorney Edward L. Dowd personally handled the case, which was moved from St. Louis after Moore's attorney claimed his client couldn't get a fair trial in St. Louis. "I guess I had it coming," Moore told a reporter after he received a sentence of eight months in the Audrain County Jail in Mexico, was fined one hundred dollars, and lost his driver's license. After Moore began the sentence, the *Globe-Democrat* reported that he was wearing blue jeans instead of prison garb and was pitching in with other prisoners to scrub the jail's floors. The paper also noted he was reading papers and books and pamphlets distributed by a church group. After spending only four months in jail, a judge put him on probation as long as he didn't go behind the driver's wheel.

Hot Rod Moore kept his word—but only in Missouri. His parole in Missouri was revoked after he got an Illinois driver's license. He fled to Chicago and disappeared, while his lawyer argued that the case against Moore was flawed. Authorities finally dropped the case, saying that Moore had already served enough time. In the early 1960s, he received more speeding tickets but nothing serious. After that, he disappeared. In 1998, Moore's brother told a reporter that Hot Rod was selling used cars somewhere in St. Charles. But the brother, Dr. Harry Moore, didn't know how to reach him. Moore's wild life in a souped-up Ford was a factor in the introduction of the point system, in which the license of anyone who accumulates a certain number of driving violation points in a specific amount of time is suspended or revoked. Fortunately, no one was injured by Moore's recklessness, unless one includes the egos of those who wanted to crack down on him.

# Owen Dacey: Dancing through His Duty

When Maestro Owen Dacey stepped up to his rostrum, an orchestra of thousands prepared to perform. On those days, the instruments weren't violas, oboes, piccolos, and contrabassoons. Instead, they were tractor-trailers, Chevys, Pontiacs, and motorcycles. Dacey wasn't a conductor but a traffic cop who brought order to unruly cabs, station wagons, and delivery trucks rushing through a bustling North St. Louis intersection right next to an exit for Interstate 70. With his feet stretched far apart, his midsection gyrating like Elvis, and his arms flailing purposefully, he danced with the skill of Fred Astaire, Michael Jackson, or Beyoncé.

"Broadway and East Grand is a man's intersection, and it takes Officer Owen Dacey to stay in the saddle there," the *Post-Dispatch* declared in 1967, four years after he started directing traffic at the corner. "With a crew of well-rehearsed drivers, Dacey gets a certain rhythm going at rush hour, a flow and tempo of traffic that reassures him and adds grace to his strenuous movements." He needed all the grace he could get. Each day, twenty thousand trucks and cars passed through the interchange.

A navy veteran who served in the South Pacific during World War II, Dacey brought those skills with him when the city police hired him in 1958. He served his entire thirty years in the department in the North Side, long enough for everyone to know him as the Dancing Policeman. Such was his knack for directing traffic that when he went on vacation, the city police dispatched two or three officers to handle the traffic he directed by himself.

In 1971, Dacey was off for two weeks after he received minor injuries when a car struck him at the intersection. While on the mend in the hospital, he received hundreds of cards from people he'd never met. And people groused that Owen Dacey's corner was going to heck in a handbasket. "They put a rookie out there, and he was all over the intersection," complained the operator of a gas station at the corner. "He didn't know where to stand. Poor guy, they ran him ragged. I wouldn't stand out there for anything." Everything was as it should be the morning Dacey returned. "Go around him, Buick, go Buick. Go, John. That's it, John," he said. "Come on, baby," he motioned to a woman motorist.

Dacey retired in 1988, but kept working one day a week as a campus police officer at St. Louis Community College at Forest Park and regularly visited Crown Candy. He died in 2009, but he forever thrashes, waves, and keeps impatient motorists at bay in videos on YouTube set to rock music. As long as he was on the St. Louis Police Department, there was no better dance floor in town than the corner of East Grand and Broadway.

# Tony Gagliarducci: Keeping Sharp on the South Side

For more than six decades in the last century, a different kind of door-to-door businessman plied the streets of South St. Louis. Anthony Gagliarducci pushed a 250-pound, two-wheel knife-sharpening cart, complete with hand-lettered sign that announced "HAND & POWER LAWNMOWERS SAWS KNIVES SCISSORS TOOLS SHARPENED." But nobody needed a sign to know that Tony Gagliarducci was in the neighborhood. An open ear was enough. "Ting tang . . . tonk . . . ting tang . . . tonk," writer Jack Maier scribbled in an article published in the old *South County Journal* in the 1980s. "Everybody in south St. Louis older than five knows that sound. 'It's Tony!' 'Here comes the scissors man!'"

Born in 1900 in a village near Naples, Italy, Gagliarducci came to America to help his brother run a bar in St. Louis. After he got here, he had a sweet time working in a candy factory and a hot time in a foundry before deciding on the life of a sharpener in 1920. So he started walking around the South Side to gather up those dull scissors and kitchen knives and restore their razor-blade edge. A blacksmith helped him fashion a pushcart complete with a seat that pulled out whenever he needed to employ the use of an attached grinding wheel. The contraption wasn't that unusual at the start. After all, through World War II and beyond, people got their milk delivered from horse-drawn milk wagons.

Before he put the edge back on his final knife, Gagliarducci would go through three of those carts, only taking off on Sunday. He was no slouch on exercise. Starting from his Bevo Mill neighborhood home at 3931 Schiller Place, he'd push the cart twenty-five or thirty miles a day. Over his career, the miles added up to nearly half a million. Those who encountered him included Stephen M. Gregali, the former alderman for the South Side's Fourteenth Ward. "I knew of him more from my childhood neighborhood. We used to walk with him and follow him on our bikes," he wrote. "He was really a nice guy. Always quick to strike up a conversation with someone in the neighborhood." When he got home, he kept himself busy sharpening push mowers.

Gagliarducci slowed in the 1980s and put an end to the grind in 1983. In 1988, he donated his third cart to the Missouri History Museum, which included it in a display with the title "Twentieth-

Century Gallery." While his death at ninety-one in 1991 ended an era, the *Post-Dispatch* and the *Suburban Journals* caught an abundance of quotes from him in feature stories about his retirement. "I sharpened as far away as Jefferson Barracks and Lemay, all over south city and some county. When the guys in the taverns heard me coming, they came out and invited me in for beer. If I drank all the beer they offered, I'd never have made my route," he said. "I sharpened these like nobody's business," he recalled. "They came, and they came, ten to fifteen of them every day." Gagliarducci's route took him about two weeks to finish, said his son, James.

"At night, he left the cart in a friend's garage or place of business, or perhaps in a garage he rented. My mother would pick him up in the car," or he would come home by bus." Tears flowed aplenty when he gave his old cart up to the Missouri History Museum. "His life and his cart," his son said, "are one and the same."

# Charles Hoessle: Snake Man

A round the time Charlie Hoessle entered school, he loved going to the St. Louis Zoo. He was in awe of the elephants and the lions and treasured the times he spent at animal shows. The chimpanzee shows were sure to bring a laugh. "It was funny to see the animals in costumes," said Hoessle, who grew up in South St. Louis. "During the war, during depression, we needed something to laugh about." But as Hoessle grew up, as he spent his life dedicated to animals, and as attitudes evolved, his views of the shows changed. In time, he would have a key role in ending the zoo's animal shows and in changing the way its animals were kept and displayed.

In third grade, bitten with curiosity about garter snakes he'd found, he checked out stacks of books about snakes from the bookmobile that came to his school. When the librarian told him he couldn't check out any more snake books, he checked out volumes on mammals and birds until he could check out the snake books again. "My mother said 'Charlie, if you would spend as much time with your school books as you do with your animal books, you might amount to something.'"

He kept up his curiosity as a Cleveland High School freshman when he brought a coffee can with a snake inside to his biology teacher. The teacher hated snakes and kicked him out of the class. So he wandered the hallways until he put the can in the open locker of a girl he was trying to impress. Soon, the girl showed up with some friends and opened the can. They screamed and got the attention of a hall monitor. Hoessle fessed up and was dispatched to the principal's office. The principal was ready to suspend the delinquent snake lover when a teacher showed up who liked him. He got the sentence reduced to probation. As for the girl he wanted to impress, "She ultimately married me in spite of it," he said.

Hoessle spent two years at the old Harris Teachers College, married the girl of his dreams, was drafted into the army, and then ran a pet store in Affton. Finally, in 1963, he got the job of his dreams: as a reptile keeper at the St. Louis Zoo. From there, he moved up the ladder at the zoo until he was named its director in 1982. Before and after, he went to exotic locations around the world to find creatures that most people would avoid. He went to Texas to collect reptiles and snakes the zoo could use to trade for animals held by other zoos. He shipped rattlesnakes to Australian zoos in exchange for pythons and monitor lizards. He traveled to Mexico to capture vampire bats. To keep them well fed, he brought outdated human blood collected by the American Red Cross. Native people in Mexico who helped him collect ground squirrels and tree squirrels loved the big sunflower seeds in wild birdseed he brought to attract the squirrels to traps. They replaced the big sunflower seeds with little ones.

The animals he brought back to St. Louis enriched the zoo, but another step he took changed it more. Under his leadership before and after he assumed the zoo's leading position, the zoo ended its animal shows and moved animals out from cramped cubicles with bars. In their place, the animals moved into more natural settings. Even though he only had two years of college when he started at the zoo, four local universities granted him honorary doctorates. Meanwhile, attendance grew until Hoessle retired in 2002 with the title of director emeritus. At eighty-five, he volunteers at the zoo, vacations with his wife, and keeps up with his children and grandchildren. Looking back, he believes much of his career was made possible by the snakes, bugs, and other animals that always were part of his life.

# Bucket Joe: The Most Famous Homeless Man in St. Louis

I t's common to see homeless people standing at busy entrances or exits to interstate highways holding a scrap of cardboard promising they'll work if somebody supplies them with food. Bucket Joe had a different approach, which thousands of South St. Louisans still remember. For decades, the disheveled, often drunken man carried buckets on or near Grand Boulevard and Gravois Avenue and made his living cleaning windows. Some remembered him swinging an old broom at passing cars at Chippewa Street and Gravois Avenue. Some smiled as they waved at Joe, others yelled in derision. But thousands of South Siders remembered him.

An unscientific survey a reporter took of regulars at a South Side senior citizen center in 2008 showed that almost everybody had heard of him. That newshawk for the old *South Side Journal* found that twelve out of fifteen of those interviewed at the Five Star Senior Center, 2832 Arsenal Street, knew about him. "It seemed like no matter where you were on the street, he was walking on Gravois," said Marie Tritschler. "My mom and dad had a bakery shop at Eighteenth and Lynch and he'd come and do the windows," said Joan Barron, another person at the Five Star Center. Many had stories to tell about Bucket Joe. But did any of them really know about Bucket Joe? Not a one. Well, there was one, and that made all the difference.

In fact, Bucket Joe was safe and happy, thanks to the kindness of a friend. In 1990, *South Side Journal* reporter Lois Kendall wrote a story revealing that the man's name was Joseph "Bucket Joe" Mossberger and that he had been living on the street since he was eighteen in the 1960s. "He lumbered up and down the sidewalks of the South Side for some thirty years, a big man with a shaved head and a loping gait. He wore raggedy dress pants chopped off at the knees and scruffed brogan shoes without socks. He rarely wore a jacket, except on the coldest days, and in either hand, he carried buckets," she wrote. He slept in alleys or empty buildings, anyplace he could find a place for his head. His diet was whatever came from a handy garbage can or what someone gave him. "He'd been hit by cars, arrested by police and incarcerated in mental institutions."

The picture was pitiable, and it would have stayed as such if it hadn't been for an old friend of Mossberger's named Clifford Cockrell. A landlord and resident of the Forest Park Southeast neighborhood, Cockrell arranged for Mossberger to have a warm bed, three meals a day, two cats, and a radio. Mossberger, who was developmentally disabled, spoke to Kendall in 1997. But when another writer sought an interview with Mossberger in 2010, Cockrell refused. As he brought his friend in from the streets, so Cockrell shielded Mossberger from what others might think about him. Bucket Joe may have washed his last window on Grand Boulevard and Gravois Avenue years ago, but he lives on in the memories of longtime South Siders.

# Bob Cassilly: An Ageless Kid on a Playground

Welcome to the mind of Bob Cassilly, where a Ferris wheel tops a ten-story building and a school bus hangs over the edge of the same building, the City Museum. In this mind, gargantuan concrete turtles inhabit a land on the other side of Interstate 64 from the St. Louis Zoo. The classically trained sculptor died in a tragic accident in 2011, but samples of how he imagined his world are everywhere in St. Louis. He added stone lions to the Gateway Mall downtown, baboons and a hippopotamus to the St. Louis Zoo, and a monarch butterfly to the Butterfly House in Chesterfield. He graced Manhattan's Riverside Park with a hippo playground and raised a three-hundred-foot-tall giraffe at the Dallas Zoo.

St. Louisans best remember Cassilly for the City Museum, a downtown multistory playground that rates with the weirdest museums in the world. Why put two abandoned planes on a museum roof? As any kid would say, because it's fun! And Bob Cassilly was a kid as much as anybody. "Bob lived by his own rules," said Rick Erwin, who worked for Cassilly for five years and is now director of the City Museum. In the City Museum, those rules dominate. "We're just doing things we did when we were kids," Erwin said. "It's a

nice place for adults to bring their kids and kind of relive their childhood." In 2015, 785,000 happy kids and wannabe kids toured Bob Cassilly's playground.

Cassilly's training for his various oddball works of art began in Webster Groves, where he assembled vines for swinging, a tree house, and a tunnel near a creek next to his yard. His mother noticed that Bob had a curious bent for whittling with a Boy Scout knife his father had given him. She took her son to Webster College sculpture teacher Rudolph Torrini, who saw in him an unusual talent. Cassilly's desire to do everything in a big way especially impressed Torrini. "He takes on things without thinking of the technical aspect. He just barges in and does it," Torrini said in 1994. Cassilly got a scholarship to the Cleveland Art Institute, but he didn't stay after he discovered he knew more than many students there. By that time, Torrini was teaching at the all-women Fontbonne College. In spite of this, Cassilly started studying with Torrini. In 1970, he became the first male graduate of Fontbonne, which is now Fontbonne University.

Over the years, Cassilly worked on major architectural and sculptural projects that brought him attention both locally and nationally. The biggest was the purchase of the former International Shoe Building at 1501 Washington Avenue in 1993 and its conversion into the City Museum. At 762,000 square feet, it finally had enough space for Bob Cassilly to play. He surrounded the parking lot with serpents and adorned a grand facade with an Egyptian queen. He installed caves, a five-story slide, and the MonstroCity jungle gym and opened the City Museum in 1997.

Visitors discover oddities like construction cranes, salvaged bridges, old chimneys, and great big metal spiders.

Cassilly could be a piece of work about his artworks. Such was the case with Turtle Playground, a collection of climbable concrete turtles, eggs, and snakes he crafted for the kiddos' pleasure on Oakland Avenue on the other side of Interstate 64 from the St. Louis Zoo. He got cheesed off in 2000 when St. Louis defiled his creations with a layer of protective resin. Soon after that, spray-painted tears appeared on the turtles' cheeks and the words "We've been slimed," and "Help" on the shells. Cassilly said he didn't know how that got there but later admitted he was responsible. Then in 2007, someone decapitated the head of the playground's giant snake. It happened right before highway workers planned to remove it before the implosion of a bridge across I-64 that the snake's head was "biting." Cassilly denied swiping it, but he gave the heads up that it was safe. He finally fessed up that he did it and later created a new snake's head.

A son of Cassilly, Max Cassilly, speculates that his father may have had attention deficit disorder and showed some mild traits of Asperger's syndrome. Whatever the case, he took on a major new project in his last years: converting the old fifty-four-acre Missouri Portland Cement plant near the Mississippi River in North St. Louis into a new attraction called Cementland. He created a cobblestone castle, gazebos fashioned from cement hoppers, a lake, beaches, and more. People said Cassilly thought it would be his masterpiece. He was operating a bulldozer on the site one day in September 2011 when it flipped over and killed him. He was sixty-one. Had he lived, he would have kept building his playgrounds. As it is, he made enough to keep kids in St. Louis busy and happy.

# Tom Dunn: River Man

Tom Dunn sits in his office in a barge floating on the Mississippi River below the Gateway Arch. On the wall around him are blowups and posters showing long-gone excursion boats. Through a window behind him, he can see barges going up and down the Mississippi. "There's an old saying, 'If you work on the river, you'll be down here the rest of your life,'" he said. That's what happened with Tom Dunn. After a taste of miserable wintertime on-deck toil on the river, he kept working on the water. Today he's continuing the long tradition of passenger traffic on the Mississippi River, as the person in charge of the two remaining St. Louis cruise boats.

Dunn's career path turned toward the river after he'd graduated from St. Louis University and spent four years working in a lab with burn patients at a hospital. He was up to a different kind of challenge and signed up as a deckhand in the blustery cold months of February and March 1972 on the Upper Mississippi and Upper Illinois Rivers. The boat was one of the first to get through the ice to St. Paul. It was really chilly. It was so chilly that the man he

replaced fell into the river and almost died from hypothermia. The job left Dunn cold, but it led him to a job as advertising and sales manager of Streckfus Steamers, which operated excursion boats in New Orleans and St. Louis. One of its vessels was the big *Admiral*, which then was in its glory days. His book, *Admiral: A Boat Full of Memories*, recounts how it went on to be an entertainment complex and floating casino before being scrapped in 2011. What's left of Streckfus is the *Tom Sawyer* and the *Becky Thatcher* tour boats, operated by Bi-State Development Agency, under the name Gateway Arch Riverboat Cruises.

Dunn's workdays vary but often include greeting visitors. His favorite question is, "How long is a one-hour cruise?" A cafe and gift shop keep him busy, as do details of the one-hour cruise, a late-night party cruise, a dinner cruise, a blues cruise, and a cruise to Kimmswick. Dunn or an employee sometimes fills bottles with river water and then places them in the gift shop, where they're sold for $2.50 each. The label gives strict instructions not to drink it. More tragically, Dunn has been involved in cases in which a dead body floats down the river close to his facility. He emphasizes that it is rare, and that there is only about one such instance a year on both sides of the river ten to fifteen miles in both directions from downtown. On the lighter side, Dunn once had to watch over a nursing duck who planted herself in one of the cruise service's jon boats to lay on her four eggs.

Dunn also must keep an eye on the water level. It could be dangerous, a nuisance, or an occasion for humor. The joke was on him when he tried to figure out how to get through water that covered the way to his office. In such cases, either a jon boat carries a person, or he walks through the water. Once, Dunn had a suit and didn't want to get the pants wet. So he wore his swimming trunks on the bottom and his blazer, shirt, and tie on top as he walked through the water. But to a TV camera crew filming his walk to work, and to viewers at home, it looked like he was wearing only his underwear.

Something more serious happened on August 1, 1993, when the Mississippi reached the high point of a record flood. At the worst time, several vessels, including a heliport, two barges containing a Burger King, and a retired minesweeper broke loose from their moorings, came downriver, and smacked into the *Tom Sawyer* and three dock barges. This potentially dangerous situation ended for the barges and the *Tom Sawyer* when they floated onto the Gateway Arch grounds, snapping a tree in the process. Towboats brought them back. When all was dry, the National Park Service billed the cruise service $5,000 for the tree. It wasn't enough to fight, Dunn recalls, so the cruise service paid the bill.

Such perils make it harder to keep river cruise boats going than businesses onshore. But Dunn is confident they'll keep going. Since the steamboat *Zebulon Pike* first reached St. Louis in 1817, the town has been a center for river traffic. Excursion boats like the *Becky Thatcher* and the *Tom Sawyer* should keep running for years to come. "We really feel that we're maintaining a St. Louis tradition," Dunn said. "To have no riverboats in St. Louis would just be unbelievable."

# Joe Edwards: How to Be *Loopish*

As a preschooler, Joe Edwards collected rocks. Then he moved on to baseball cards, comic books, and records. Thousands of records, enough to cause any normal parent to cry, "Stop it already, we're running out of space." Fortunately, "I had very, very understanding parents who didn't throw things out like most peoples' parents," Edwards said. "My record collection grew into one of the largest in the United States." At one time, he had thirty thousand forty-five RPM records and eighteen thousand seventy-eight RPM records. Edwards still collects things, but of a different sort. He collects revived buildings and successful businesses in the mega-trendy Delmar Loop district, as well as the praise of the American Planning Association for being one of the ten great streets in America.

The Delmar Loop was far from a destination in 1972, when Edwards opened a bar and restaurant at 6504 Delmar Boulevard, in part because he wanted a location for his various collections. He

named it Blueberry Hill, after an iconic Fats Domino song. Now the Delmar Loop is six blocks on both sides of the St. Louis–University City line and attracts people from everywhere. In 1972, it was anything but that. The rent on Delmar was low, but only because the area had badly declined. Motorcycle gangs came regularly. The people Edwards wanted to attract stayed away. But he struggled and persisted. He almost went out of business more than once in the first two years because he banned about two-thirds of his potential customers from entering. One factor that helped was the jukeboxes that played records from his collection. They garnered national attention. Among his customers—then and now— was Affton native and future movie star John Goodman. "He and his friends had such a good time. They would pump quarter after quarter in the jukebox," Edwards said.

Eventually, Edwards's efforts paid off and set a tone for his business and the area. He also quickly realized that to survive, he had to organize the area. Over time, the plan worked. Doing his  part, he bought seventeen to twenty buildings and found himself in possession of several businesses. He owns the Tivoli Theatre and the building that houses it. He opened such Delmar Loop destinations as the Pin-Up Bowl, the Flamingo Bowl, the Peacock Loop Diner, and the Moonrise Hotel. With seating for two thousand, the Pageant has been judged as one of the five best concert venues in the world. A more intimate setting is the Duck Room in a basement area below Blueberry Hill. With room for 340 people, it was the scene of monthly concerts by St. Louis's own Chuck Berry from 1996 to October 2014, during the week of Berry's eighty-eighth birthday. Edwards first connected with Berry when he wanted to put the rocker on a can of brew he'd produced, called Rock 'n' Roll Beer.

The planned Delmar Hall will have seating for about eight hundred, a midpoint between the Pageant and the Duck Room. "Bands are really excited about it because they love playing in the Loop," Edwards said.

Bringing growth to the Loop partly involves boring matters like building consensus in an area and figuring out whether to renovate a building or put up something new. But then the question comes: "What are the types of businesses that would be *Loopish?*" One unquestionably Loopish thing is the man-made moon on top of the Moonrise Hotel. It weighs a ton and a half and is ten feet in diameter, which Edwards claims makes it the world's biggest thing like that. You'll have to trust him, but Edwards did a really thorough Internet search and couldn't find anything bigger. He likes whimsical, fun places. "I try to create a place where people can put their troubles aside for a while."

Edwards has had one idea after another, but one of his biggest brainstorms may have come during a 1997 meeting about what to do about the area of Delmar east of Skinker Boulevard. It was obvious to him: a 2.2-mile vintage trolley connecting the Delmar Loop to Forest Park. Nobody at the meeting liked the idea. But he persisted and gained the support, the location, and the local and national cash needed to make the dream come true. When completed in the spring of 2017, the $51 million project could bring more people to see Edwards's collections in Blueberry Hill and other places he owns. Those coming to Blueberry Hill can view a real stuffed lion, an old poster advertising an appearance by Chuck Berry, a Pac-Man room featuring all kinds of Pac-Man stuff, and displays of memorabilia for the Cardinals, the Simpsons, and so much more. The collections are the kind of things that make parents proud, as long as they don't have to store them.

# George Simon: Patriarch of the Mangoes and Pears

It's Saturday afternoon at the Soulard Market, and that means it's showtime for George Simon. "I got a bag of grapes for a dollar," he says, next to his produce stand in the market's southeast wing. "We'll give you two broccoli for a dollar," he said, amidst the mangoes, bananas, eggplants, sweet potatoes, and zucchinis. His wrinkles offer hints that he's worked at the market in eight decades and owned a stand there for six. His tone seems gruff at first, but it's quickly clear that it's wrapped in smiles. "I like people, to talk to them," he said, "to make 'em laugh." His voice is full of gravel and sounds right out of the Bronx. Actually, he started much farther away than New York City.

Simon arrived in St. Louis from Lebanon in 1947 with his mother, father, brother, and sister. He immediately went to work at the Inserra Brothers' stand at the Soulard Market. "We needed money," he said. "There was five of us." He won't say his age, but he noted that when he arrived in

St. Louis, he was placed in the third grade at Madison School in South St. Louis. "Then a priest came over to our house, and he said, 'Why do you go to public school?'" When told that the family didn't have any money, the priest arranged for him to go for free to St. Mary of Victories school at Third and Gratiot Streets. He graduated in 1952 and attended McBride High School. While there, he met his future wife, Marilue, and learned that his brother had been killed in the Korean War. After he graduated from high school in 1956, he married Marilue and started his own stand in the 1960s.

Over time, the Simons had ten kids, all of whom spent time helping out. His daughter Brenda Winebright, who is in her late fifties, recalls starting when she was eight. At the time, she said, she was just a little kid, not yet understanding but learning a lot. The ten kids grew up and gave George and Marilue Simon thirty-eight grandkids. Each of them gets a chance to stack tomatoes and oranges on Saturdays, if they feel like coming. "A grandparent never puts pressure on a grandchild. He loves to be around them," Simon said. He shows that affection with a large paper picture of those grandkids posted on the wall behind the stand.

Among those who gaze at that photo as they stop at the stand are people who have been buying their salad makings from Simon for decades. "They bring their kids, grandkids, third generation," Simon said. Those who have known Simon for many years include Roy Wheelock, who is in his late sixties. "I came down here as a baby," he said. "Simon's got lots of stories. In fact, he'll manufacture one right on the spot." Rosina Inserra-Meyer has known him for as long as she can remember. Inserra-Meyer, who is in her late fifties, recalled that Simon worked for her father. "He is dedicated. He's got a laid-back personality, but he's not a pushover. He's always happy, no matter what." she said. "He'll always listen to whatever you have to say. He'll always bring something good out of it. He's very caring and giving, and it's so obvious that he just loves people, and they love him."

Inserra-Meyer may know about Simon's generosity, but Darryl Spinks has experienced it. "He's a good old man. He doesn't turn anyone away," said Spinks, who has helped out at Simon's stand for about a decade. If people don't have money for food, Simon will give it to them, said Spinks, who is related to the Spinks family of boxing fame. "I was homeless, and he helped me." If it's up to Simon, he'll keep selling fruits and vegetables at the Soulard Market as long as he can. His age, whatever it is, doesn't seem to matter to him. Said Simon: "I don't care. I'm just a kid."

# Albert Watkins:
# Toe Smasher at Law

When Walt Disney Productions came out with movies about a dog named Santa Paws, three writers of children's books about a dog with the same name decided Disney had gone too far. They barked to Albert Watkins, a legal beagle who specializes in David-versus-Mouse cases. The Clayton lawyer got his paws on the case and sued Disney. In hearings in federal court in St. Louis, Watkins posted a Santa Claus outside the courthouse to support the authors. Watkins lost the case, so he couldn't say he kicked Disney's butt. But he did defend the college student who sold "The South Butt" T-shirts as a parody of a better-known brand called the North Face. The North Face Apparel Co. sued and eventually got the student to stop selling South Butt products and publicizing them on social media. "Everyone knows the difference between a face and a butt," was the battle cry.

It's all in a day's work for Watkins, who's often used laughter as a tool for fighting for his clients since he hung out his shingle as a St. Louis lawyer in the late 1980s. He has collected a multitude of enemies since then, but the words "self-centered, egotistical, and a self-proclaimed expert in all matters," didn't come from any of them. Instead, they're on the website for his law practice, Kodner Watkins LC. He's been brash and a pain in the south butt ever since he was senior class president and valedictorian at Ladue Horton Watkins High School. That should have been enough for Watkins to get into Brown or Yale Universities, his family's two preferred schools. But he once was suspended for looking the wrong way at a fellow student after being told not to do it. Another time, a cleated athletic shoe he had thrown at a fellow swim team member struck the principal instead, cleats first. When he apologized, an obscenity emerged from his mouth. The principal wrote a letter with his applications to Brown and Yale saying Watkins was an aggressive student, but that sometimes his aggressiveness pointed in the wrong direction. Both schools rejected Watkins. So he went to St. Louis University and got his undergraduate degree in theology and political science and then his law degree.

Albert Watkins went into law by accident. Somebody rear-ended the car his grandmother had given him. The other driver's insurance company wouldn't pay up. "That provided sufficient impetus to get a law degree," he said. After he finished law school and passed his bar exam, he lined up a different job than the law, working for the Federal Reserve Bank in Washington, D.C. But before he started, he got a three-month defense lawyer job. He lost every case in that time, but he got the bug. He passed on the job in Washington and instead started the law firm he now leads.

Watkins soon developed a knack for taking on high-profile cases. In 1995, he defended a St. Louis city elementary school principal named James E. Strughold who faced multiple charges of sexually abusing children at his school. A jury found him innocent of sixteen felonies but guilty of six misdemeanors. Watkins appealed and got a retrial, in which Strughold was acquitted of all charges. More recently, former St. Louis Cardinals slugger Albert Pujols sued former Cardinals player Jack Clark after Clark said in a local radio talk show that Pujols was a "juicer," another word for a player who uses a performance-enhancing drug. In a letter to Pujols's lawyer, Watkins noted that "juicing" and "performance-enhancing drugs" have multiple meanings and suggested a settlement without any payment. In the end, Clark issued a statement apologizing for the remark and saying he had no knowledge of Pujols ever using an illegal or banned performance-enhancing drug. Pujols accepted the apology and dropped his suit.

Early in 2016, Watkins spent much time with reporters and on local radio talk shows talking about the controversial plans of a client, the Social House II, to open a restaurant in the Delmar Loop staffed with mostly topless female servers covered with body paint. For Watkins, it was just one more of the reasons he's become such a controversial figure. He accepts the role and says that if he's doing his job, "You are inevitably going to be stepping on toes and causing upheaval and havoc." Indeed, Watkins seems to have the gift of inducing maximum discomfort to the foot's outer reaches.

# Raynard Nebbitt: That Guy on the Overpass

For decades, Raynard Nebbitt has stood regularly on the overpass above Interstate 44 and waved at passing semis, cars, and trains on a track that runs on the north side of the interstate. Motorists, truck drivers, and train engineers returned the waves with headlight flashes, honks, and whistles. Almost everybody loved it, and why not? Nothing brightens the day like the sight of a smiling man waving at you as you drive down the road. But not everybody did, and the objections led to a special honor for the resident of northern Webster Groves.

Nebbitt started hanging around the overpass about thirty years ago, said his sister, Kathy Nebbitt. Raynard Nebbitt, who is considered a higher functioning mentally challenged person, regularly rides his bike to his job at Industrial Aid, a sheltered workshop in St. Louis. In months when the days are longer, he comes home, naps, does his chores, and heads out to the bridge until dark. When the days shorten, he heads to the bridge first, to

make sure he doesn't miss his time on the overpass. He's treated the overpass like he would his own home. If there's trash or broken glass, he's cleaned it up. "Raynard was fascinated by bridges and towers. He would build towers" said Kathy Nebbitt. "We don't know why he chose that bridge. We've been asking him." To show his sense of ownership, he cleans the overpass regularly. "He has his own shovel, his own bridge."

Everything went fine until 2005, when a neighbor who lived next to the overpass objected. Not to Nebbitt, but to all the honks and whistles meant for him from the passing cars, trucks, and trains. A nurse who worked nights, she said it prevented her from sleeping during the day.

After speaking to the nurse's husband, Kathy Nebbitt sent a letter to the editor of the *Webster-Kirkwood Times* giving her view of what was going on. The paper was soon filled with letters of support. One resident, Theresa Wojak, decided it was time to act. "He is the kindest, purest spirit—just a gentle man," said Wojak. "We thought maybe some good could come out of a little bit of the sadness." That quickly led to a petition to name the overpass for Raynard Nebbitt. Numerous attendees at an ice cream social signed. Residents were ready to sign when Kathy Nebbitt stopped by their houses. Motorists were asked to ease the tension by skipping the honks and just waving at Raynard Nebbitt when they passed under the bridge.

So it was that family and friends and Nebbitt came to a meeting of the Webster Groves City Council in June 2005 with petitions containing the signatures of more than 360 people asking that the overpass be named for Raynard Nebbitt. Today, on either side of the bridge, is a sign that says "Raynard Nebbitt Crossing." It shows that a person doesn't have to be important to receive such an honor, only to be loved. And in Webster Groves, and on Interstate 44, people do love Raynard Nebbitt.

# Bill Christman: An Artiste and a Jokester

It's easy to find where Bill Christman lives. Strut over to the Skinker-DeBaliviere neighborhood and look for the eight-and-a-half-foot-tall fiberglass white chicken out front. If Christman's clucking about, tramp to his sculpture park next door and see how old junk never looked so good. Rest on a park bench while the head of an old Big Boy statue towers over your shoulder. Gaze in awe at the "robots" scattered about made out of spare parts, or the twenty-foot-tall man's head called "the Phony Tough Guy," who holds a cigarette in its mouth. Now motor over to the corner of South Jefferson Avenue and Cherokee Street for a tacky delight: Christman's thirteen-foot-tall statue of an Indian. Add base and headdress, and the creation is twenty-one feet tall.

It's hardly high art. That's fine with Christman, who knows all the techniques of the artist but would rather have fun employing them. He's spent his career making one and all smile with his signs, sculptures, and satirical creations and nearly two decades showing them off at the City Museum. "In the high art world, humor is considered a contaminant," said Christman, a low-art type who's dedicated his life to spreading that

contaminant. He has the heart of an artiste but the mind of a jokester.

Christman's eyes led him to his life's work. They're hypersensitive. He started life around Waterman and Union and then moved to Clayton. He graduated from St. Louis University High School but still was able to become a goof-off and anarchist during his school years. He majored in sculpture and minored in art history and English at the University of Missouri in Columbia. Then he got serious, or at least as serious as somebody like Bill Christman could get.

In 1972, he was a founding partner in Blueberry Hill, Joe and Linda Edwards's venture in the Delmar Loop. He left the partnership and later went to work painting theatrical scenery at the Muny. He considers that hands-on experience the real start of his education. During the off-season, he made material for Busch Gardens and repainted backdrops for Masonic temples made in St. Louis after the World's Fair. In 1976, he started his own studio, specializing in signs, sculptures, and scenery. He stayed there for twenty years, as he married, raised a family, and developed his style.

In 1996, a friend made an offer that changed his life. Bob Cassilly, who was building a reputation locally as a rising young artist, asked for his help in a major new project, the City Museum. Cassilly gave him about six thousand square feet to build out his own Museum of Mirth, Mystery, and Mayhem. The museum opened in 1997 with the tone of a tacky roadside carnival. In eighty-hour weeks for the seven months before the museum opened in 1997, he struggled like Michelangelo painting the ceiling of the Sistine Chapel to create an exhibit scrutinizing the mystical properties of the corn dog. He painstakingly crafted another display featuring the world's largest pair of men's underpants. The text next to that exhibit declared that 98 percent of men had worn underpants over the head, either as youngsters or as drunken college students.

Christman developed his museum with the late Joe Ouellett. Ouellett was the namesake for Joe's Cafe, a properly tacky small concert hall Christman runs in the first floor of the two-story brick storefront where he lives with his wife, Mary. The couple lived on the second floor from 1980 to 1986 but moved to a home in University City to raise their kids. They moved back to the building's second floor in 2016. From the middle years of the first decade of the new millennium to the present, he came back to work on his sculpture garden.

Christman believes his wife and family kept him grounded. She thinks he's quirky and the most creative person she's ever met. "He has a very deep spiritual bent on what he does," she said. At one of the city's New Year's Eve First Night celebrations, he showed that perspective, with the Guiltorama, in which a person confessed to a taxi driver, priest, or hairdresser and then was assigned a punishment, like a whipping with a narrow piece of foam rubber. Then the judged got a soda jerk hat with such titles as "Redeemed," "Unrepentant," or "Sinner." A theologian might tut-tut the show, saying it made light of a serious subject. But that's what Bill Christman does.

# Paul "Father Time" Pagano: Everyone's Goodwill Ambassador

E verything Paul Pagano does is designed to bring a smile. As "Father Time," he's happy enough to shake the hands of whomever he encounters at fairs, outside baseball games, holiday parades, and wherever more than two or three folks are gathered in and around St. Louis. The work grew out of his reaction to a personal tragedy but became a blessing for the whole region. Those who've seen him wearing his red, white, and blue hat next to a delivery truck with a sign saying "Father Time Says God Bless America" since 1981 may have numbered in the millions.

"I'll tell you, I'm like an old landmark of the city of St. Louis," Pagano said one day in January 2016 in his room at the Delmar Gardens North assisted living center in Florissant. He wore an American flag tie and his red, white, and blue hat. At ninety-two, he gets around in a scooter-wheelchair. But he's as sharp as ever. "When I was a little boy, Kate Smith, you know of her, she used to sing on KMOX," he said, mentioning the singer known for her renditions of "God Bless America." Back then, he lived around Jefferson and Cass Avenue. "My mother used to turn it on, and I always did love that song, 'God Bless America.'"

He grew up, cleared minefields for the army during World War II, had seven kids, and spent his life driving a produce truck. In 1979, his happy life seemed to end when his wife, Mary, died. He spent two years after that lamenting his loss and then decided it was time to break free. He dressed up as Father Time for a Halloween party. He played the harmonica at nursing homes. And he started going to events with his red, white, and blue miniature school bus–produce delivery van covered with messages of cheer. He was out every weekend, "summer months, especially," he said. "I usually had my bus decorated with flags and different sayings. I had two speakers in front and two in the back," Pagano said.

"Why did I like it? I liked everything about it," he said. "I didn't smoke or drink, but I loved to get out and do my acting." Depending on the sports venue he was standing outside, Pagano would wear hats exclaiming "Go Cards," "Go Rams," or "Go Blues." People spotted him at the Italian Fest in Collinsville, Fair St. Louis, and Dogtown's St. Patrick's Day Parade. Motorists driving by Ashby and St. Charles Roads in St. Ann often saw him, dressed in red, white, and blue. And he got married again, to a woman named Mary Schwab, who was patient enough to allow him to continue his garish hobby. She's now with him at Delmar Gardens North.

Not everything went well for this messenger of cheer. At the end of the 1990s, his neighbors in unincorporated St. Louis County west of Overland noticed him selling vegetables from time to time out of the colorful mini school bus–delivery van he brought to events. The county said that was illegal in residential areas and spent a year trying to get him to stop. Finally, he went to court and said he wouldn't do it anymore. He donated the bus to the American Cancer Society's vehicle auction program and kept going.

In his eighties, Pagano slowed down, but people still remembered him. He went into Delmar Gardens North. "For a long time, a lot of people didn't know my real name. They'd address me as Father Time." On Pagano's ninetieth birthday, Mayor Francis Slay issued a proclamation noting the date. He stays close to his eighteen grandchildren and his ten great-grandchildren. His son John Pagano makes sure he's still around and about. About a dozen times a year, John takes his father to parades and events where he can greet the crowds from his scooter wheelchair. At the start of 2016, John said he hoped to take his father to more. It's a delight for both Paul Pagano and those he greets. One couple told John Pagano that when they used to go to Cardinal games, they would go first to the Stan Musial statue and then to greet Father Time before going into Busch Stadium. "They come up to him, and it's like their childhood," John Pagano said. So it is that one man's fight against grief brought joy to thousands.

# Steven Fitzpatrick Smith: Weatherman

O n the last day of January 2016, Steven Fitzpatrick Smith stood outside his bar at 3132 South Kingshighway Boulevard and faced a tiny camera attached to a small drone. "It's a little windy, but it's a great day to drink outside," he said, a newsboy's cap firmly on his head, as he began his South Kingshighway weather report. As the small helicopter rose, the viewer on the computer saw the sign identifying the watering hole as the Royale. "As you can tell, there are people drinking in the courtyard. It's warm, probably in the low sixties, maybe." The drone weather report was one of many Smith has recorded, which have been viewed thousands of times on the Royale's Facebook page since he started shooting them toward the end of the first decade of the twenty-first century. It's one of numerous methods he employs to pack customers in at what he calls a different kind of public house.

Many customers are political types, which in St. Louis generally means Democrats. "Most of the politicians are pretty aware of the place, and senators come here." In 2008 and again in 2016, the Royale sponsored a mock Iowa Democratic caucus. Barack Obama won the caucus in 2008, while Bernie Sanders was the big winner in 2016. It was in keeping with the history of the establishments that occupied the building before Smith started the Royale more than a decade ago. Governors frequented it when local politician Fred Colombo owned it from the 1920s to the 1950s. He named the place Colombo's, but Smith called his the Royale partly in homage to the French name of the road out front.

Kingshighway was originally known as Rue de Roi. Smith also thought of a couple of Delta 88 Royales he has owned.

At forty-three, Smith has thirty years in the bar business and even more time in business. When he was about six and living in Chicago, he wanted to shine shoes in that city's downtown. His dad said he was too young, and that was that. When he was older and living in Kirkwood, he hawked more than a hundred copies a day of the *Post-Dispatch* as a newsboy. By reading writers like Clarence Page and Elaine Viets in those papers, he developed a lifetime love of newspapers.

"At thirteen, I started washing dishes in a basement bar in Webster Groves," said Smith, who finished his teenage years in the South Side. "My sister worked there, so I guess they turned a blind eye to it," he said. His father tended bar, and his mother was a stewardess. "So we had that service in our blood," he said.

Later, he often worked at bars and events because he was a big guy. "I doubled as a bouncer," he said. Once the crowd got unruly at a concert at a downtown bar. He told everybody to go fight outside. When they were outside, he locked the doors.

The different upbringing notwithstanding, Smith graduated from St. Louis University High School in 1991 and from St. Louis University in 1996. His bachelor's degree was in history, but a career in serving the people with entertainment, food, and drink was ahead. Smith managed events for the *Riverfront Times* and the City Museum and worked in the underwriting department for KDHX Radio. He also found himself in the rough-and-tumble world of boxing as a boxer, coach, and promoter for his Panda Athletic Club. The specialty was something called the Hoosierweight Boxing Championships. But the main event was trouble.

"I had the head of the local boxing commission threaten me a few times," he said. Then–Missouri attorney general Jay Nixon issued a cease-and-desist order to stop a match. After negotiations, the match went on. That didn't stop the threats. "The guy who was threatening me had gone to jail for breaking somebody's legs," Smith said. He survived by looking over his shoulders and always eating with his back against the wall. He more or less ended his involvement in boxing after 2005, when he opened the Royale.

Since then, Smith has involved himself in less dangerous activities. He's staged events with themes like a Cuban Missile Crisis Party and debates on local issues. He's always tried to do the best for customers but sometimes has failed. "I had a dream of having a floor-length urinal, and I was going to make a huge investment of rehabbing my bathrooms," Alas, the city denied the request because there wasn't access to a trap below. "I thought about talking to a lawyer, but I decided to pick my battles." So it is that men raising a glass at the Royale can't take a break in front of a floor-length urinal. But they'll have a good time in other ways and will know the weather before they come.

# JIM MERKEL: EPILOGUE

## My Wasted Life as a Writer

When I was young, I decided to spend my life writing. I would be much better off today had I chosen something useful, but tell that to a headstrong kid. I mention this because Josh Stevens at Reedy Press wanted me to write an epilogue saying why I deserve a place with the others in this book. I could write about many things, but the story about how I've frittered away my life at a keyboard should do it.

Early on, I banged on a toy typewriter, then honed my skill at high school and college newspapers. Inspired by the importance of the people's right to know in the Watergate era, I latched onto a journalism degree from the University of Missouri at Columbia. In the real world, my job wasn't as exciting as Dustin Hoffman and Robert Redford made it seem in *All the President's Men.* In the small Pennsylvania town of Sunbury, I covered debates about the best bids for road salt in rural townships and wrote detailed analyses of the year's tomato crop. I once let a coworker write about the explosion in a dryer at a coin-operated laundry that happened when I accidentally threw a spray can in with my wet underwear.

Then I tried my hand as a freelance writer. In this world of free enterprise, I scribbled articles for *Grit* on such important matters as a horse-drawn milk wagon in Niagara Falls, New York. Subscribers to this publication were within reach of kids who read ads in comic books about prizes they'd get by selling *Grit.* The now-defunct United States Information Agency assigned me to craft tomes about such bits of Americana as Little League baseball and the powerful leader of the Republican Party in Williamsport, Pennsylvania. The idea was to convince readers of my articles in other countries what a wonderful place America is. I was doing my part to fight commies. A couple of dozen times I penned short articles for the *New York Times* about real estate in small Pennsylvania towns. I went to a community, wrote the story, called a phone number, and dictated it into a tape recorder. This was years before e-mail. Then came constant calls from editors demanding specifics about the square footage of a planned mall, which stores would be in the mall, what opponents said and what this said about the town's real estate climate. Before I finished, I'd made dozens of calls for more information. For this, I received two hundred dollars plus expenses. By the hour, I didn't make much on this or anything else.

My wife, Lorraine, and I survived this period, but barely. We learned the meaning of scrimping and trusting in the Lord, Who was trying to get me to do something that actually made money. Lorraine made wondrous cheap meals like soybean pie, a yummy pizza-like concoction made with soybeans, cheese, tomato sauce, and a cornbread crust. When I really needed cash, I did consulting jobs, like cleaning toilets. No wonder I returned to newspaper reporting after eight years.

I wound up at the *Press-Enterprise* in Bloomsburg, Pennsylvania, a tough paper known for attacking government wrongdoing and leaning on wimpy reporters like me who didn't want to ask questions that caused politicians to scream at them. So prodded, I wrote a story saying a district attorney hadn't paid his property taxes. His wife sent me a letter saying my article was wicked. The whole town seemed to hate me. Fortunately, not every article made the world mad at me. I spent months faking—er, writing—the paper's cooking articles. Then somebody in a club made up of people who really knew about cooking asked me to speak to their group. I declined and admitted I knew nothing about cooking.

The paper was a great place. But we had different things in mind. In 1991, we quit our jobs and headed back to St. Louis. I found work at the *Suburban Journals of Greater St. Louis*, while

Lorraine did office work. The *Suburban Journals* covered news others ignored, like the guy with the collection of ten thousand bottle caps. Then in May 2013, we got the news that I and almost every other reporter at the Journals no longer had a job.

We've scraped by since this forced retirement. But I did find more time for something that's come to dominate my life. It started in 2009, when Reedy Press publisher Josh Stevens asked me to compile stories I'd written about the South Side into a book, which became *Hoosiers and Scrubby Dutch: St. Louis's South Side.* Josh changed my life. No, I'd say he ruined it, or at least any chance of living a normal life. At 3 a.m., I go to my laptop to write sentences that just came into my mind. I'm always at a library or archive, reading some fifty-year-old newspaper article or interviewing somebody for the next nugget.

While everybody else is relaxing, I'm writing to make my Sunday night weekly deadline. Those confounded endless deadlines. I write with the conviction that the only way to make progress with a book is to write so much every week without fail. If the floodwaters are rising to the second floor, my priority is driving with my laptop and notes to a Starbucks on high ground. If there's space in the car for Lorraine and the cat, great. But only if it doesn't stop me from meeting my deadline.

A person will always be a murderer even though he's only killed one person. That's how it is with books. Write one book, and you're always an author. *Hoosiers and Scrubby Dutch* should have been enough. But I plowed on with *Beer, Brats, and Baseball: German-Americans in St. Louis* and *The Making of an Icon: The Dreamers, the Schemers, and the Hard Hats Who Built the Gateway Arch.* I provided text for a coffee table book, *Unique Homes of St. Louis.* Then Josh asked me to do this volume, and I kept on. I won't stop. I'm intent on nothing less than mass authorship. It's all Josh's fault. He's okay, for an editor. But he's still an editor. Every editor I've known has told me my brilliant writing is unreadable blather, and I need to fix it. A voice inside says editors are the reader's only defense against having to plow through a mass of mush masquerading as sentences and paragraphs. But since I'm as headstrong as when I started writing, I tell that voice to shut up.

A couple of times I fixed things so I was the editor. In 2001, I self-published a travel book about the lighthouses in our favorite vacation spot, Lake Superior's Apostle Islands. Lorraine's task was proofreading. After going through the book about eight times, she declared, "I hate this book!" For more than eight thousand dollars, we bought 4,400 books. The book sold about a thousand copies, and we somehow only lost about four thousand dollars. We still have dozens of boxes of books. Lorraine vowed she wouldn't let me do that again. It didn't stop me, though, from self-publishing a novel in 2015. It was through something called print on demand, in which you order as few copies as you want. Lorraine didn't scream as much about this relatively small expense, but I suspect she would have been happy if I hadn't done it. Setting yourself up in business to print and sell one's own books can be rewarding. But the way I see it, authors haven't arrived until they sign a contract with a real publisher. Besides that, they pay for printing, not me. Lorraine likes that.

I guess all that makes me a colorful character, but it takes work and the right genes to reach this pinnacle. Fortunately, I come from a family of colorful characters. One family story relates how my great-uncle Sam walked into a store and tried on a pair of gloves. As a stunned clerk watched, Uncle Sam pulled out a scissors and lopped off one of the glove's fingers. It turned out Uncle Sam was missing a finger at the part of the glove he removed. Then there was grandma, known to all as Crazy Granny. When her '57 Chevy reached a stop light, she halted by jamming on her brakes, while keeping her other foot on the gas. When the light turned green, she removed her foot from the brake, showing that the stories about the power of a '57 Chevy were true.

Mine isn't the only family with, um, interesting members. I suspect many St. Louisans come from colorful families and that St. Louis has a higher CCPTQ (Colorful Characters Per Thousand Quotient) than any other place in this here United Colorful States of America. It seems that way to anybody who's been around this town for a while. People with drive or sense abandon our city for burgs on the move, like Dallas or Atlanta. Those who remain must be oddballs, or seem so, since all we want is a slower pace and for all conversations with new acquaintances to begin with the words, "So where did you go to high school?" We consider having a few more characters around as a reasonable price for being in a place that's just more comfortable. *Post-Dispatch* columnist Bill McClellan summed up the way we feel when he said, "We are the only city in the world that has a memorial to honor those who left." Let others leave. I'll take our colorful characters any day.

# ACKNOWLEDGMENTS

Newspapers, the saying goes, are the first draft of history. I didn't know how true this adage was until I started writing books about St. Louis. Time and time again, I'd find myself poring over old articles in the clippings file in the St. Louis Room of the Central Library downtown. I'd hear the clacking of manual typewriters in the hands of masters of the language, making so many colorful characters of our town come alive. In my research for this book, I read hundreds of those articles. They made history come alive. The *St. Louis Post-Dispatch* and newspapers.com deserve thanks for developing a database of every article the paper has ever printed, going back to 1874. The act of typing "Marlin Perkins," or "Bill Veeck" immediately yielded wonderful details about the city's colorful characters that otherwise were lost without an immense search through microfilm. To the talented newspaper writers who provided so many delightful details for the stories herein, I dedicate this listing of acknowledgments.

As always, many people helped to make this volume possible. Among them are the crew in the Central Library's St. Louis Room and its Rare Book and Special Collections Department and the Missouri History Museum Library and Research Center. I mustn't forget my friend of fifty years, Joseph Winkler, the retired manager of research collections at the St. Louis Public Library. The Collinsville Historical Museum was especially helpful in providing information for my essay on Dakin Williams, the brother of Tennessee Williams. The Buder Branch of the St. Louis Public Library offered some fine places for writing in the many times I wanted to get out of the house. So did numerous local coffee shops. My favorite is Hartford Coffee Company south of Tower Grove Park. Come by and you might see me, typing away.

Josh Stevens at Reedy Press did a terrific job in developing the concept for this book and patiently providing advice to improve each of these tales. The same goes for Barb Northcott, Elizabeth Terry, Don Korte, and everybody else in the Reedy crew. Thanks go as well to the more than sixty people who opened up their schedules for interviews, short or long. I can say the same for the authors of the fifty or so books cited in this book, as well as the writers of the many authoritative websites I consulted. My apologies go to the many I've overlooked in this list of people deserving thanks.

As always, my greatest thanks go to Lorraine, the woman who has stayed with me through thirty-six wonderful years of marriage. She is always loving, always patient, always supportive, and always forgiving when I spend too much time in front of the computer writing my books. She was especially helpful when she pitched in to do indexing and proofreading of this manuscript. As always, no typo or confusing phrase stands a chance in a manuscript she's perused. Love you, honey.

After Lorraine, I give my greatest thanks to you, my readers. This is the fourth book that includes such a message. I feel the need to express such a message more than ever. Over time, I've learned that a writer is successful when someone he doesn't know tells him he got a few hours of enjoyment from reading one of his books. I'm humbled to say many have said that to me. I hope you get the same pleasure from this book. That will mean the many hours I've spent writing it were well spent.

# SOURCES

## Introduction

"Obsession." Merriam-Webster online thesaurus. http://www.merriam-webster.com/thesaurus/obsession. Accessed June 14, 2016.

## William Reedy: A *Mirror* to St. Louis

Kirschten, Ernest. *Catfish and Crystal: The Story of St. Louis.* New York: Doubleday, 1960.

Putzel, Max. *The Man in the Mirror: William Marion Reedy and His Magazine.* Cambridge, Massachusetts: Harvard University Press, 1963.

Sandweiss, Lee Ann, ed. *Seeking St. Louis: Voices from a River City, 1670–2000.* St. Louis: Missouri Historical Society Press, 2000.

Stevens, Josh. Interview. August 21, 2015.

*St. Louis Post-Dispatch.* March 30, 1897; July 28, 1920; July 29, 1920.

## Bill Mauldin: Point Man for the Soldier

DePastino, Todd. *Bill Mauldin: A Life Up Front.* New York: W.W. Norton & Co., 2008.

## Robert Hyland: The Boss Who Never Slept

Absher, Frank. Interview. October 23, 2015.

Grundhauser, Paul. Interview. October 25, 2015.

*Riverfront Times.* March 11–17, 1992.

*St. Louis Post-Dispatch.* May 13, 1979; May 14, 1979; March 6, 1992; March 8, 1992.

## Dana Brown: Tiger Hunter, Coffee Seller

Dana Brown Charitable Trust. http://danabrowncharitabletrust.org/bio.html. Accessed December 22, 2015.

"Still Brewing the World's Richest Coffee." *St. Louis Commerce.* October 1979, December 1988.

*St. Louis Post-Dispatch.* July 1, 1958; April 30, 1978; October 22, 1994; November 13, 1994.

## Don "Johnny Rabbitt" Pietromonaco: Bruno and Friend

"A Walk Down Memory Lane with Ron Elz." Ladue News, http://www.laduenews.com/living/special-features/a-walk-down-memory-lane-with-ron-elz/article_94eef656-0aea-5514-b3e9-e47540764360.html. Accessed August 15, 2016.

Absher, Frank. Interview with follow-ups. March 15, 2016.

*Billboard*. January 17, 1976.

Connell, Bud. Interview with follow-ups. March 15, 2016.

"Elz, 'Johnny Rabbitt,' Ron." CBS St. Louis KMOX Johnny Rabbitt, http://stlouis.cbslocal.com/personality/johnny-rabbitt/. Accessed August 15, 2016.

King, Jonnie. Interview. March 2016.

Neeley, Tim. Information sheets e-mailed to author. March 18, 2016.

Neeley, Tim. Interview with follow-ups. March 14, 2016.

St. Louis Media History Foundation, http://www.stlmediahistory.org/index.php/Radio/RadioHOFDetail/elz-ron. Accessed August 15, 2016.

*St. Louis Post-Dispatch*. April 29, 1962; April 30, 1962; May 20, 1962; April 4, 1963; March 4, 1964; July 12, 1964; July 15, 1966; October 6, 1968; February 16, 1979; April 20, 1997.

## Amadee Wohlschlaeger: Fifty-Nine Years a Weatherbird

Martin, Dan. Interviews.

Reidenbaugh, Lowell, Craig Carter, ed., Amadee Wohlschlaeger, ill. *The Sporting News Take Me Out to the Ball Park*. St. Louis: Sporting News Publishing Co., 1983.

*St. Louis Post-Dispatch*. March 21, 1991; May 23, 1991; June 6, 1991; March 18, 1992; April 8, 2001; June 25, 2014; June 29, 2014.

## Jack Carney: The Broadcasting King of St. Louis

Carney, John. Interview. April 5, 2016.

"Jack Carney." St. Louis Media History Foundation, http://www.stlmediahistory.com/index.php/Radio/RadioHOFDetail/carney-jack. Accessed April 11, 2016.

*St. Louis Post-Dispatch*. December 10, 1972; April 12, 1981; November 29, 1984.

## William Barnaby Faherty, SJ: A Wordsmith to the End

*Jesuit Bulletin.* March 1979.

*St. Louis Globe-Democrat.* November 18–19, 1978; January 25, 1980; May 28–29, 1983.

*St. Louis Post-Dispatch.* November 2, 1978; September 30, 1990; August 15, 2000.

Waide, John. Interview. October 15, 2015.

## Steve Mizerany: The King of Schmaltz

Merkel, Jim. *Hoosiers and Scrubby Dutch: St. Louis's South Side.* St. Louis: Reedy Press, 2014.

*Profile St. Louis.* September 7, 1977.

*St. Louis Globe-Democrat.* June 27–28, 1981.

*St. Louis Post-Dispatch.* April 16, 2011.

## Miriam Blue: Sound Advice from a Cleaning Lady

Absher, Frank. Interview. October 23, 2015.

St. Louis Media History Foundation. http://www.stlmediahistory.org/. Accessed October 23, 2015.

*St. Louis Post-Dispatch.* December 7, 1975; April 20, 1983.

UPI. "Miriam Blue, a cleaning lady who became a radio . . .," http://www.upi.com/Archives/1983/04/20/Miriam-Blue-a-cleaning-lady-who-became-a-radio/3160419662800/. Accessed October 23, 2015.

## Dave Sinclair: Grandma's Car Dealer

Dave Sinclair Auto Group. http://davesinclair.com/. Accessed May 22, 2016.

Merkel, Jim. *Hoosiers and Scrubby Dutch: St. Louis's South Side,* 2nd ed. St. Louis: Reedy Press, 2014.

"President Bush Announces Start of Iraq War." https://www.youtube.com/watch?v=5BwxI_l84dc. Accessed May 22, 2016.

Sinclair, Dave. "Ford 50th Anniversary." https://www.youtube.com/watch?v=rPxJ92HzpAI. Accessed May 22, 2016.

Sinclair, Dave. Interview with Jennifer Blome on KSDK. https://www.youtube.com/watch?v=zsk0FqHzCbI. Accessed May 20, 2016.

Sinclair, Dave. "I Sell American Cars." https://www.youtube.com/watch?v=UYww4E1-Zoo.

*St. Louis Post-Dispatch.* December 27, 2003; September 26, 2009.
United States Department of Labor, Bureau of Labor Statistics. Monthly
  Unemployment Rates, 2006–2016. Accessed May 22, 2016.

## Carl Hepp: High Art on Cable Access
Allen, Karen. Interview and follow-up, February 10, 2016.

## Fred Teutenberg: A Man and His Chicken
"Dirt Cheap Big Game Commercial." https://www.youtube.com/
  watch?v=vs4QCyP2QB4. Accessed January 13, 2016.
"Dirt Cheap Chicken Breaks out of the Shell." https://www.youtube.com/
  watch?v=vs4QCyP2QB4. Accessed January 13, 2016.
"Dirt Cheap Commercial." https://www.youtube.com/
  watch?v=r1jbS6VJYEU. Accessed January 13, 2016.
Ferrick, Elizabeth, and Joannie Dalrymple. Interview. Date unknown.
*St. Louis Post-Dispatch.* March 29, 2000; April 9, 2004; November 2, 2009;
  January 1, 2015.

## Elaine Viets: She Kills Us
"Elaine Viets." http://elaineviets.com/. Accessed May 13, 2016.
"Elaine Viets." Wikipedia, https://en.wikipedia.org/wiki/Elaine_Viets.
  Verified by Elaine Viets, May 9, 2016. Accessed May 13, 2016.
"Pen, Ink, and Crime, Sisters in Crime, New England, Not Quite Twenty
  Questions for Elaine Viets." https://sincne.wordpress.com/2014/07/31/
  not-quite-twenty-questions-for-elaine-viets/. Accessed May 17, 2016.
*St. Louis Post-Dispatch.* March 1, 1987; January 27, 1991; January 11, 1994;
  January 27, 1994; Sept. 22, 1994; March 20, 1996.
Viets, Elaine. Interview and speech at Spencer Road Branch, St. Charles
  City-County Library. May 9, 2016.

## Pete Parisi: TV for the Rejects
Merkel, Jim. *Hoosiers and Scrubby Dutch: St. Louis's South Side,* 2nd ed.
  St. Louis: Reedy Press, 2014.

## Mike "King of Credit" Stein: Comic by Accident

"Schweig Engel Ghostbusters ad." https://www.youtube.com/ watch?v=2t8sxeJYpEc. Accessed January 16, 2016.

Stein, Mike. Interview with follow-ups and correspondence. January 16, 2016.

## Ray Hartmann: Twice in a Lifetime

Hartmann, Ray. Interview with follow-ups and correspondence. November 16, 2015.

KSDK.com. http://archive.ksdk.com/news/article/183773/0/Martin-Duggan-saying-farewell-to-KETCs-Donnybrook. Accessed November 19, 2015.

stlmag.com. http://sites.stlmag.com/slm_media_group/aboutus.html. Accessed November 19, 2015.

St. Louis Media History Foundation. "Ray Hartmann." http://www. stlmediahistory.com/index.php/Print/PrintHOFDetail/hartmann-ray. Accessed November 20, 2015.

*St. Louis Post-Dispatch*. October 9, 1988; May 28, 2015.

## Amanda Doyle: She Ain't Boring

Doyle, Amanda. *100 Things to Do in Saint Louis Before You Die*. St. Louis: Reedy Press, 2013.

Doyle, Amanda. Interviews with follow-up correspondence. January 6 and 8, 2015; June 16–21, 2016.

Doyle, Amanda, Kerri Bonasch, and Don Korte. *Finally, A Locally Produced Guidebook by and for St. Louisans*, 2nd ed. St. Louis: Reedy Press, 2014.

Doyle, Amanda, and Tony Waters, ill. *To The Top! A Gateway Arch Story*. St. Louis: Reedy Press, Jefferson National Parks Association, 2012.

Metropolis St. Louis. http://www.mstl.org/index.php. Accessed January 10, 2016.

## Mickey Carroll: Gateway City Munchkin

*St. Louis Post-Dispatch*. March 20, 1980; March 23, 1981; May 8, 1989; April 23, 1992; August 23, 1999; November 29, 1999; May 7, 2004; October 10, 2004; May 8, 2009; April 24, 2014; May 17, 2014.

## Harry Fender: Mom Complex

"Harry 'Captain 11' Fender." Find a Grave, http://www.findagrave.com/cgi-bin/fg.cgi?page=gr&GRid=48895557. Accessed October 29, 2015.

"KPLR Station History." http://kplr11.com/contact/station-history/. Accessed October 29, 2015.

Magazine article from unidentified source and date in clipping filing in Special Collections Department of Central Library, St. Louis Public Library.

*St. Louisan*. December 1976.

*St. Louis Globe-Democrat*. December 4, 1960.

*St. Louis Post-Dispatch*. December 19, 1949; July 13, 1980; June 4, 1995.

*St. Louis Star-Times*. May 9, 1951.

## Joe Besser: The Stooge from St. Louis

Besser, Joe, with Greg Lenburg and Jeff Lenburg. *Once a Stooge, Always a Stooge*. Santa Monica, California: Roundtree Publishing, 1988.

*St. Louis Post-Dispatch*. March 3, 1988.

## Davey Bold: A Nose for Comedy

"It Looks Like Rain in Cherry Blossom Lane," https://www.youtube.com/watch?v=gKE2xTFfaKc. Accessed June 18, 2016.

"Jimmy Durante." http://www.biography.com/people/jimmy-durante-9282022. Accessed February 20, 2016.

*St. Louis Post-Dispatch*. January 28, 1972; February 10, 1975; July 18, 1978; March 30, 1989.

"Wernher Von Braun." http://www.biography.com/people/wernher-von-braun-9224912. Accessed February 20, 2016.

## Marlin Perkins: TV's First Man of Animals

"Marlin Perkins' Snake Bite." snopes.com, http://www.snopes.com/radiotv/perkins.asp. Accessed August 26, 2015.

"Marlin Perkins: St. Louis Zoo." http://www.stlzoo.org/about/history/marlinperkins/.

*New York Times*. June 15, 1986.

Perkins, Marlin. *My Wild Kingdom: An Autobiography*. New York: E. P. Dutton, 1982.

*St. Louis Globe-Democrat*. April 4, 1962; April 17, 1962; September 5, 1962; November 7, 1963; December 7–8, 1963; March 8, 1970.

*St. Louis Post-Dispatch.* January 2, 1929; October 26, 1955; June 18, 1958; February 24, 1961; April 3, 1962; April 16, 1962; April 17, 1962; January 4, 1963; November 6, 1963; December 7, 1963; July 18, 1967; September 28, 1969; March 29, 1970; June 15, 1986.

## Phyllis Diller: Funny Lady

Corrigan, Patricia. Interview. April 7, 2016.

Diller, Phyllis, with Richard Buskin. *Like a Lampshade in a Whorehouse.* New York: Penguin: 2005.

"Phyllis Diller at the Bar." https://www.youtube.com/watch?v=Uw470J8qpEo. Accessed June 8, 2016.

"Phyllis Diller: *Goodnight, We Love You* [Highlights]." https://www.youtube.com/watch?v=FP0mXwcIQEU. Accessed June 11, 2016.

*New York Times.* August 20, 2012.

"Phyllis Diller with Groucho Marx on *You Bet Your Life.*" https://www.youtube.com/watch?v=YnzT46uTQ0s. Accessed June 8, 2016.

"Stephanie Diller Waldron." Find a Grave, http://www.findagrave.com/cgi-bin/fg.cgi?page=gr&GRid=115373843. Accessed April 10, 2016.

*St. Louis Post-Dispatch.* December 11, 1960; November 26, 1961; October 25, 1987; August 12, 2012.

## Slim Cox: Down Home on the South Side

Hardcastle, Sharon. Interview. March 13, 2016.

Merkel, Jim. *Hoosiers and Scrubby Dutch: St. Louis's South Side,* 2nd ed. St. Louis: Reedy Press, 2014.

*St. Louis Post-Dispatch.* October 30, 2014.

## Stan Kann: Vacuum Man

Gasko, Tom. Interview. February 5, 2016.

Merkel, Jim. *Hoosiers and Scrubby Dutch: St. Louis's South Side,* 2nd ed. St. Louis: Reedy Press, 2014.

## Miles Davis: Deep Freeze of Cool

Bessières, Vincent, and Franck Bergerot. *We Want Miles: Miles Davis Versus Jazz.* New York: Skira Rizzoli, 2010.

Carner, Gary. *The Miles Davis Companion: Four Decades of Commentary.* New York: Schirmer Books, 1996.

Davis, Miles, with Quincy Troupe. *The Autobiography*. New York: Touchstone, 1989.

Maher, Paul, Jr., and Michael K. Dorr. *Miles on Miles*. Chicago: Lawrence Hill, 2009.

*New York Times*. September 29, 1991.

Rock and Roll Hall of Fame. "Miles Davis Biography." https://rockhall.com/inductees/miles-davis/bio/. Accessed January 23–24, 2016.

*Rolling Stone*. "Miles Davis, Biography." http://www.rollingstone.com/music/artists/miles-davis/biography. Accessed January 23–24, 2016.

Stevens, Josh. Correspondence. January 25, 2016.

*St. Louis Post-Dispatch*. September 30, 1991; May 14, 2001.

## Charlotte Peters: The First Lady of St. Louis TV—and Corn

Schwartz, Patricia Peters. *Charlotte!: The First Lady of Saint Louis Television*. St. Louis: Triangle Publishing, 1994.

*St. Louis Globe-Democrat*. June 1, 1967; July 18, 1967; July 11, 1970.

*St. Louis Post-Dispatch*. May 20, 1956; January 28, 1962.

## Redd Foxx: Junk Man

Acham, Christine. *Revolution Televised: Prime Time and the Struggle for Black Power*. Minneapolis: University of Minnesota Press, 2005.

*New York Times*. October 13, 1991.

"Redd Foxx." Find a Grave, http://www.findagrave.com/cgi-bin/fg.cgi?page=gr&GRid=2704. Accessed April 30, 2016.

"Redd Foxx: The Official Site." Biography, http://www.reddfoxx.com/about/biography.html. Accessed April 28, 2016.

Starr, Michael Seth. *Black and Blue: The Redd Foxx Story*. Milwaukee: Applause Theater and Cinema Books, 2011.

*St. Louis Post-Dispatch*. September 28, 1973; April 21, 1974; October 13, 1991.

*St. Louis Today*. September 28–29, 1973.

"St. Louis Walk of Fame, Redd Foxx." http://www.stlouiswalkoffame.org/inductees/redd-foxx.html. Accessed April 30, 2016.

"Teacher Serve: The Trickster in African American Literature." http://nationalhumanitiescenter.org/tserve/freedom/1865-1917/essays/trickster.htm. Accessed July 11, 2016.

## Pokey LaFarge: Guitar Pickin' for America

Collar, Matt. "Pokey LaFarge." http://www.allmusic.com/artist/pokey-lafarge-mn0002092058/biography.

Dunham, Nancy. "Pokey LaFarge Laments Labels, Defends America's Heartland." *Rolling Stone*, April 3, 2015. http://www.rollingstone.com/music/features/pokey-lafarge-laments-labels-defends-americas-heartland-20150403. Accessed March 26–28, 2016.

LaFarge, Pokey. "Central Time" lyrics. http://www.songlyrics.com/pokey-lafarge/central-time-lyrics/. Accessed May 10, 2016.

LaFarge, Pokey. Correspondence to author. April 11, 2016; May 10, 2016.

LaFarge, Pokey. Interview. March 24, 2016.

LaFarge, Pokey. *Marmalade*. http://www.allmusic.com/album/marmalade-mw0001566875. Accessed May 10, 2016.

LaFarge, Pokey. "Something in the Water." Pokeylafarge.net, https://www.youtube.com/watch?v=FXzEVLSoVqw. Accessed May 10, 2016.

National Public Radio. "Pokey LaFarge: Tiny Desk Concert." NPR, http://www.npr.org/event/music/135508843/pokey-lafarge-tiny-desk-concert. Accessed March 28, 2016.

Pokey LaFarge. http://www.pokeylafarge.net. Accessed various dates, Spring 2016.

## Chris Von der Ahe: No *Dummkopf*

Broeg, Bob. *Bob Broeg's Redbirds: A Century of Cardinals' Baseball*, rev. ed. St. Louis: River City Publishers, 1987.

Cash, Jon David. *Before They Were Cardinals: Major League Baseball in Nineteenth-Century St. Louis*. Columbia, Missouri: University of Missouri Press, 2002.

"Chris Von der Ahe." Bellefontaine Cemetery, http://bellefontainecemetery.org/historical-story/chris-von-der-ahe/. Accessed November 27, 2015.

Golenbock, Peter. *The Spirit of St. Louis: A History of the St. Louis Cardinals and Browns*. New York: Avon Books, 2000.

Hetrick, J. Thomas. *Chris Von der Ahe and the St. Louis Browns*. Lanham, Maryland: The Scarecrow Press, 1999.

Merkel, Jim. *Beer, Brats, and Baseball: German-Americans in St. Louis*, 2nd ed. St. Louis: Reedy Press, 2015.

## Sam Muchnick: Mr. Wrestling

"Chase Park Plaza, History." http://www.chaseparkplaza.com/our-rich-history-1. Accessed October 31, 2015.

"Historic Hotels of America: Chase Park Plaza." http://www.historichotels.org/
 hotels-resorts/chase-park-plaza/history.php. Accessed October 31, 2015.

Matysik, Larry. *Wrestling at the Chase: The Inside Story of Sam Muchnick and the
 Legends of Professional Wrestling*. Toronto: ECW Press, 2005.

"Nicholas II." http://www.biography.com/people/nicholas-ii-21032713.
 Accessed October 31, 2015.

*St. Louis Post-Dispatch*. June 11, 1995; December 31, 1998; January 4, 1999.

## Dizzy Dean: Dizzy with Delight

Allen, Lee. *Dizzy Dean: His Story in Baseball*. New York: G. P. Putnam's Sons,
 1967.

Baseball Almanac. http://www.baseball-almanac.com. Accessed February
 13–15, 2016.

Baseball-Reference.com. http://www.baseball-reference.com. Accessed
 February 13–15, 2016.

"Dizzy Dean." http://www.dizzydean.com/biography.htm. Accessed May 21,
 2016.

Heidenry, John. *The Gashouse Gang: How Dizzy Dean, Leo Durocher, Branch
 Rickey, Pepper Martin, and Their Colorful Come-from-Behind Ball Club Won
 the World Series—and America's Heart—During the Great Depression*. New
 York: Public Affairs Books, 2007.

Mueller, Carolyn E., and Ed Koehler, ill. *Dizzy Dean and the Gashouse Gang*.
 St. Louis: Reedy Press, 2015.

## Bob Broeg: The Happy Sports Scribbler

"Bob Broeg, 87, Dubbed Stan Musial 'The Man.'" Associated Press, October
 29, 2005. Boston.com, http://www.boston.com/news/globe/obituaries/
 articles/2005/10/29/bob_broeg_87_dubbed_stan_musial_the_man/.
 Accessed December 20, 2015.

Broeg, Bob. *Memories of a Hall of Fame Sportswriter*. Champaign, Illinois:
 Sagamore Publishing, 1995.

Broeg, Bob. *The 100 Greatest Moments in St. Louis Sports*. St. Louis: Missouri
 Historical Society Press, 2000.

Cosgrove, Ben. "Appreciating Stan 'The Man' Musial and the Best Nickname
 in Sports." *Sports Illustrated*, http://www.si.com/mlb/2015/06/23/
 stan-musial-man-nickname-cardinals. Accessed December 15, 2015.

Marecek, Greg. Interview. December 2, 2015.

Miklasz, Bernie. "Remembering Bob Broeg." Football Writers Association of America, http://www.sportswriters.net/fwaa/news/2005/broeg051029. html. Accessed December 17, 2015.

*St. Louis Post-Dispatch.* June 4, 2000; October 29, 2005.

"St. Louis Sports Hall of Fame Class of 2013." Bob Broeg Media, http:// www.stlshof.com/index.php?option=com_content&view=article&id=33 &Itemid=222. Accessed December 20, 2015.

## Gussie Busch: Crown Prince of the Redbirds

"August A. Busch Jr. 'Gussie' Highlights Video." https://www.youtube.com/ watch?v=cZqSCBNYCTg. Accessed April 14, 2016.

Baseball-Reference.com. "St. Louis Cardinals Team History and Encyclopedia." http://www.baseball-reference.com/teams/STL/. Accessed April 16, 2016.

"Dedication to Our Craft." Anheuser-Busch, http://anheuser-busch.com/ index.php/our-heritage/history/. Accessed April 17, 2016.

Garrison, Chad. "Busch Unbound: Divulging Secrets from the Sudsy to the Sordid, a New Book Pops the Top off St. Louis' Beer-Brewing Dynasty." *Riverfront Times*, November 8, 2012. http://www.riverfronttimes. com/stlouis/busch-unbottled-divulging-secrets-from-the-sudsy-to-the-sordid-a-new-book-pops-the-top-off-st-louis-beer-brewing-dynasty/ Content?oid=2501601. Accessed May 11, 2016.

Grant's Farm. www.grantsfarm.com. Accessed April 16, 2016.

"Gussie Busch." Society for American Baseball Research, http://sabr.org/ bioproj/person/ca6d5e2d. Accessed April 15–17, 2016.

Hernon, Peter, and Terry Ganey. *Under the Influence: The Unauthorized Story of the Anheuser-Busch Dynasty.* New York: Simon & Schuster, 1991.

Merkel, Jim. *Beer, Brats, and Baseball: German-Americans in St. Louis,* 2nd ed. St. Louis: Reedy Press: 2014.

*New York Times.* September 30, 1989.

*St. Louis Post-Dispatch.* May 29, 1954; September 30, 1989; October 3, 1989.

Unreal. "Busch Family Mishaps: The Cocktail Pairings." *Riverfront Times,* May 1, 2011. http://www.riverfronttimes.com/foodblog/2011/01/05/busch-family-mishaps-the-cocktail-pairings. Accessed May 15, 2016.

## Bill Veeck: When Bill Veeck Came to Town

Baseball-Reference.com. "Baltimore Orioles Team History and Encyclopedia." http://www.baseball-reference.com/teams/BAL/. Accessed November 29, 2015.

Baseball-Reference.com. "Bill Veeck." http://www.baseball-reference.com/bullpen/Bill_Veeck. Accessed November 27–28, 2015.

Baseball-Reference.com. "Cleveland Indians Team History and Encyclopedia." http://www.baseball-reference.com/teams/CLE/. Accessed November 27, 2015.

Baseball-Reference.com. "St. Louis Cardinals Team History and Encyclopedia." http://www.baseball-reference.com/teams/STL/. Accessed November 29, 2015.

Broeg, Bob. *Memories of a Hall of Fame Sportswriter*. Champaign, Illinois: Sagamore Publishing, 1995.

Broeg, Bob. *The 100 Greatest Moments in St. Louis Sports*. St. Louis: Missouri Historical Society Press, 2000.

Corbett, Warren. "Bill Veeck." Society for American Baseball Research, http://sabr.org/bioproj/person/7b0b5f10. Accessed November 27, 2015.

Eskenazi, Gerald. *Bill Veeck: A Baseball Legend*. New York: McGraw-Hill, 1988.

Mackreth, Bob. Correspondence. November 30, 2015.

Merkel, Jim. *Beer, Brats, and Baseball: St. Louis Germans*. St. Louis: Reedy Press, 2010.

Veeck, Bill, with Ed Linn. *Veeck as in Wreck*. Chicago: University of Chicago Press, 2001.

## Yogi Berra: The Phenom of Elizabeth Avenue

Baseball Almanac. "Yogi Berra Stats." http://www.baseball-almanac.com/players/player.php?p=berrayo01. Accessed December 3, 2015.

Berra, Yogi, with Dave Kaplan. *You Can Observe a Lot from Life by Watching: What I've Learned about Teamwork from the Yankees and Life*. Hoboken, N.J.: John Wiley & Sons, 2008.

Berra, Yogi, with Dave Kaplan. *When You Come to a Fork in the Road, Take It!: Inspiration and Wisdom from One of Baseball's Greatest Heroes*. Waterville, Maine: Thorndike Press, 2001.

*St. Louis Post-Dispatch*. September 23, 2015.

"Yogi Berra." National Baseball Hall of Fame, http://baseballhall.org/hof/berra-yogi. Accessed December 3, 2015.

## Bob Uecker: Bob Uecker Blows His Horn

"1994—Bob Uecker." https://www.youtube.com/watch?v=bJ0rIYl4w6Y.

Baseball Almanac. "Bob Uecker Quotes." http://www.baseball-almanac.com/quotes/quouec.shtml. Accessed March 14, 2016.

Baseball-Reference.com. "Bob Uecker." http://www.baseball-reference.com/players/u/ueckebo01.shtml. Accessed December 2, 2015.

"Bob Uecker." Society for American Baseball Research Biography Project, http://sabr.org/bioproj/person/ed8fc873. Accessed December 2, 2015.

Marecek, Greg. Interview with follow-ups. December 2, 2015.

Uecker, Bob. *Catcher in the Wry: Outrageous but True Stories of Baseball.* New York: Jove Books: 1986.

## Mickey Garagiola: The Important Garagiola Brother

Matysik, Larry. *Wrestling at the Chase: The Inside Story of Sam Muchnik and the Legends of Professional Wrestling.* Toronto: ECW Press, 2005.

Merkel, Jim. *Hoosiers and Scrubby Dutch: St. Louis's South Side,* 2nd ed. St. Louis: Reedy Press, 2014.

*St. Louis Globe-Democrat.* June 15, 1974.

*St. Louis Post-Dispatch.* July 23, 1998; August 31, 2010.

## Zip Rzeppa: Life after the Zippos

Rzeppa, Zip. *For a Greater Purpose: My Life Journey.* St. Louis: Mater Media, 1999.

Rzeppa. Zip. Interview with follow-ups. December 24, 2015.

"Billy Joel—'Root Beer Rag.'" https://www.youtube.com/watch?v=RmLqhhqbYGU. Accessed January 3, 2016.

"The Zippo Awards (Friday, January 13, 1989)." https://www.youtube.com/watch?v=1VmAS4zt9YM. Accessed January 3, 2016.

## Ernie Hays: The Music Man of Busch Stadium

Hays, Loreta. Interview. May 1, 2016.

Hays-Hogstrom, Pam. Interview. May 1, 2016.

Marecek, Greg. Interview. April 29, 2016.

*St. Louis Post-Dispatch.* April 25, 1985; September 30, 1989; September 29, 2002; September 30, 2010; November 2, 2012.

## Josephine Baker: No Friend of St. Louis

Baker, Josephine, and Jo Bouillon. *Josephine.* New York: Marlowe & Company, 1977.

Haney, Lynn. *Naked at the Feast: A Biography of Josephine Baker.* New York: Dodd, Mead & Company, 1981.

Lahs-Gonzales, Olivia, ed. *Josephine Baker: Image and Icon*. St. Louis: Reedy Press, 2006.
"La Revue Nègre." http://users.dickinson.edu/~laurent/french365d/images/right_01.html. Accessed January 2, 2016.
*St. Louis Globe-Democrat*. December 10, 1937.
*St. Louis Post-Dispatch*. January 21, 1958; February 21, 2001; February 19, 2003; February 5, 2012; April 20, 2014.
*St. Louis Star-Times*. March 6, 1951.
*Time*. October 21, 1935.

## Dick Gregory: Laughing at Racism

Gregory, Dick, with Robert Lipsyte. *Nigger*. New York: E. P. Dutton and Co., 1964.
*St. Louis Globe-Democrat*. November 26, 1961.
*St. Louis Post-Dispatch*. March 12, 1961; January 28, 1968; July 5, 1992; February 25, 2001; January 30, 2003; August 3, 2008.

## Father Dismas Clark: Priest to the Unwanted

Cargas, Harry J. "The Hoodlum Priest: RIP, the Story of Fr. Dismas Clark, S.J." In *The Homiletic and Pastoral Review*, January 1964.
*New York Times*. April 3, 1961; August 11, 1989.
*Parade*. February 26, 1961.
*St. Louis Globe-Democrat*. November 29, 1959; March 2, 1961; March 6, 1961; August 10, 1963.
*St. Louis Post-Dispatch*. August 15, 1963.

## Percy Green: Master of Outrage

Green, Percy. Interview. February 2, 2016.
"Percy Green on St. Louis's Veiled Prophet." https://www.youtube.com/watch?v=4m2Fe_tER5Y. Accessed February 7, 2016.
*Riverfront Times*. October 19–25, 1988; June 28, 2000.
*St. Louis American*. November 4, 2015.
*St. Louis Globe-Democrat*. January 17, 1970.
*St. Louis Post-Dispatch*. July 12, 1970.
*South Side Journal*. September 30, 2001; October 10, 2001.
"The Root of the Veiled Prophet Parade in St. Louis, Missouri." https://www.youtube.com/watch?v=RGezOLQ-BVg. Accessed February 7, 2016.
"Veiled Prophet Organization." http://www.veiledprophet.org/videos. Accessed February 7, 2016.

## Larry Rice: Stubborn for Good

"History of NLEC." http://historyofnlec.newlifeevangelisticcenter.org/. Accessed June 7, 2016.

Rice, Chris. Interviews. August 11, 2015; August 21, 2015; June 6, 2016; et al.

Rice, Larry. Interviews. August 11, 2015; August 22, 2015; June 8, 2016; et al.

Siedhoff, Bill. Interview. June 1, 2016.

*St. Louis Post-Dispatch.* April 13, 1989; December 11, 2014; December 9, 2015; January 5, 2016; January 6, 2016; April 27, 2016.

## Randy Grim: He Speaks for the Dogs

Grim, Randy. Interview. October 1, 2015.

Roth, Melinda. *The Man Who Talks to Dogs: The Story of Randy Grim and His Fight to Save America's Abandoned Dogs.* New York: Thomas Dunn Books, 2004.

*St. Louis Post-Dispatch.* May 12, 2012.

Stray Rescue. http://www.strayrescue.org/. Accessed October 3, 2015.

## Eric Brende: Doing Better by Doing Without

Brende, Eric. Interview with follow-up correspondence and interviews. April 24, 2016.

## Cbabi Bayoc: Masterpiece for the Dads

"365 Days with Dad | Cbabi Bayoc | TEDxGatewayArch." https://www.youtube.com/watch?v=elvQl9c3FI8. Accessed May 15, 2016.

Bayoc, Cbabi. Interview. May 11, 2016.

Boucher, Brian. "Artists Activate in Response to Ferguson Shooting." *Art in America.* http://www.artinamericamagazine.com/news-features/news/artists-activate-in-response-to-ferguson-shooting/. Accessed May 19, 2016.

Fowler, Nancy. "St. Louis Artist Cbabi Bayoc's '365 Days with Dad' Draws to Close." St. Louis Public Radio, http://news.stlpublicradio.org/post/st-louis-artist-cbabi-bayoc-s-365-days-dad-draws-close. Accessed May 11, 2016.

Lee, Trymaine. "Race and Class with a Side of Cupcakes in Ferguson." MSNBC, http://www.msnbc.com/msnbc/race-and-class-side-cupcakes-ferguson. Accessed May 19, 2016.

*St. Louis Post-Dispatch.* August 30, 2014.

TED. https://www.ted.com. Accessed May 19, 2016.

"The Artist as Entrepreneur, Cbabi Bayoc." http://www.umsl.edu/continuinged/artist/artist-interview-cbabi.htm. Accessed May 11, 2016.

## Daniel "Boone" Fuller: The Vigil of Daniel "Boone" Fuller

"Billboard Sitter Ends Vigil as St. Louis Notches Another Murder." http://www.stltoday.com/news/local/crime-and-courts/billboard-sitter-ends-vigil-as-st-louis-notches-another-murder/article_7a0256b2-6c5c-5a58-9ed4-2ff8e4ee9e92.html. Accessed November 8, 2015.

"'Draw Muhammad' Billboard Defaced in North St. Louis." *Riverfront Times*, June 23, 2015. http://www.riverfronttimes.com/newsblog/2015/06/23/draw-muhammad-billboard-defaced-in-north-st-louis. Accessed November 8, 2015.

Fuller, Daniel "Boone." Interviews with follow-up calls. November 3–4, 2015.

Metropolitan Police Department, City of St. Louis, Missouri, Crime Statistics page, http://www.slmpd.org/crime_stats.shtml. Accessed August 14, 2016.

## Rev. Kenneth McKoy: Walking to Stop the Killing

McKoy, Kenneth. Interview with follow-up conversations. May 25, 2016.

"Nightlife." Facebook page.

## Thomas Hart Benton: Guns, Politics, and a Dying Man's Vote

"Andrew Jackson, 1767–1845: A Brief Biography." http://www.let.rug.nl/usa/biographies/andrew-jackson/. Accessed June 15, 2016.

Chambers, William Nisbet. *Old Bullion Benton: Senator from the New West: Thomas Hart Benton, 1782–1858*. Boston: Little, Brown, and Company, 1956.

Faherty, William Barnaby, S.J., assisted by NiNi Harris. *St. Louis: A Concise History*. St. Louis: The Masonry Institute of St. Louis, 1999.

"Senator Thomas Hart Benton." State Historical Society of Missouri Historic Missourians, http://shsmo.org/historicmissourians/name/b/bentonsenator/. Accessed June 15, 2015.

Smith, Elbert B. *Magnificent Missourian: The Life of Thomas Hart Benton*. Philadelphia, New York: J. P. Lippincott, 1958.

*St. Louis Post-Dispatch*. April 18, 2010.

## Bryan Mullanphy: The Eccentric Philanthropist

Hyde, William, and Howard J. Conard. *Encyclopedia of the History of St. Louis, Vol. III.* New York, Louisville, St. Louis: The Southern History Co., 1899.

*St. Louis Globe-Democrat.* February 29–March 1, 1964.

*St. Louis Star-Times.* Clipping of unknown date from files of St. Louis Public Library's Central Library.

Travelers Aid International. http://www.travelersaid.org. Accessed September 24, 2015.

Van Ravenswaay, Charles. *St. Louis: An Informal History of the City and Its People, 1764–1865.* St. Louis: Missouri Historical Society Press, 1991.

## Edward Gardner Lewis: Born for the Shell Game

Atascadero Chamber of Commerce. http://www.atascaderochamber.org/. Accessed October 2, 2015.

City of Atascadero. http://www.atascadero.org/. Accessed October 2, 2015.

*St. Louis Globe-Democrat.* August 27, 1950.

*St. Louis Magazine.* February 1964.

Straight, David L. "Order No. 10–Post Office Protection of the Express Cartel." http://postalmuseum.si.edu/symposium2011/papers/Straight-Order_No_10.pdf.

*Sunset Magazine.* September 1925; October 1925; November 1925; December 1925; January 1926.

University City. http://www.ucitymo.org/. Accessed September 30, 2015.

## Red Villa: Barkeep Alderman

Merkel, Jim. *Hoosiers and Scrubby Dutch: St. Louis's South Side.* St. Louis: Reedy Press, 2010.

*St. Louis Post-Dispatch.* December 8, 1990.

Villa, Matt. Interview with follow-up correspondence and interviews. August 2015.

Villa, Thomas. Interview. August 2015.

## James Eagan: The Green Man of Florissant

*St. Louis Post-Dispatch,* September 5, 1963; September 12, 1963; March 15, 1974; January 17, 1975; March 11, 1986; March 29, 1999; November 4, 2000; November 5, 2000.

## Bill Bangert: The World's Strongest Mayor

"Bill Bangert." BoxRec, http://boxrec.com/media/index.php/Bill_Bangert. Accessed August 14, 2016.

*New York Times.* February 17, 1952; February 20, 1952.

*Riverfront Times.* February 14, 2001.

*St. Louis Post-Dispatch.* February 4, 1947; April 13, 1950; May 8, 1952; February 10, 1954; October 5, 1954; April 24, 1956; November 1, 1985; July 15, 2011.

## Dakin Williams: In His Brother's Shadow

"Brother of Tennessee Williams Left Nothing in $10 Million Estate." United Press International, March 4, 1983. http://www.upi.com/Archives/1983/03/04/Brother-of-Tennessee-Williams-left-nothing-in-10-million-estate/7299415602000/. Accessed January 31, 2016.

Brown, Dennis. "Do Not Inter (and Other Misconceptions about Tennessee Williams' Relationship with His Brother Dakin)." *Riverfront Times,* August 27, 2008. http://www.riverfronttimes.com/stlouis/do-not-inter-and-other-misconceptions-about-tennessee-williams-relationship-with-his-brother-dakin/Content?oid=2453604. Accessed January 30, 2016.

*Collinsville Herald.* November 6, 1972; September 19, 1977; May 11, 1981.

*Collinsville Herald-Journal.* April 6, 1989; December 12, 1993; November 2, 1997; May 25, 2008; undated article in the files of the Collinsville Historical Museum.

Cuthbert, David. "Theater Guy: Remembering Dakin Williams, Tennessee's 'Professional Brother' and a Colorful Fixture at N.O.'s Tenn Fest." http://blog.nola.com/davidcuthbert/2008/05/theater_guy_remembering_dakin.html. Accessed January 30, 2016.

"Stevenson, Adlai Ewing III, (1930–)." *Biographical Directory of the United States Congress,* http://bioguide.congress.gov/scripts/biodisplay.pl?index=s000890. Accessed January 30, 2016.

*St. Louis Post-Dispatch,* May 21, 2008.

*Sunday Journal* (East St. Louis, Ill.). March 3, 1963.

Undated article circa February 1968 in the files of the Collinsville Historical Museum.

*Wall Street Journal.* Undated article in the files of the Collinsville Historical Museum.

## Mickey McTague: Master of the Laugh Line

McTague, Margaret. Interview. December 17, 2015.

Merkel, Jim. *Hoosiers and Scrubby Dutch: St. Louis's South Side,* 2nd ed. St. Louis: Reedy Press, 2014.

*St. Louis Globe-Democrat.* August 27–28, 1966; September 9–10, 1967.

*St. Louis Post-Dispatch.* December 21, 2011; December 29, 2011.

## Bill Haas: Don Quixote in St. Louis

Bill Haas campaign website. votebillhaas.com. Accessed October 11, 2015.

Brennan, Charlie. Interview. July 29, 2016.

Haas, Bill. Interviews with follow-up interviews and correspondence. October 8 and October 10, 2015.

*St. Louis Post-Dispatch.* April 1, 1992; June 6, 1992; January 5, 1997; February 11, 1997; April 17, 1997; April 23, 1997; July 27, 1997; November 13, 1997; February 7, 2001; October 12, 2001; June 20, 2004; January 26, 2005; January 30, 2005; February 17, 2005; February 24, 2005; October 22, 2010.

## Beatle Bob: He Never Stops Dancing

Friss, John. Interview. March 9, 2016.

Matonis, Bob (Beatle Bob). Interview. March 9, 2016.

Scheel, Jason. Interview. March 9, 2016.

Stevens, Ron. Interview. March 11, 2016.

*St. Louis Post-Dispatch.* March 6, 2016.

## John Smith T: The Gentleman Duelist

Darby, John F. *Personal Recollections of John F. Darby.* St. Louis: G. I. Jones and Company, 1880.

"The Treason Trial of Aaron Burr." http://law2.umkc.edu/faculty/projects/ftrials/burr/burraccount.html. Accessed September 26, 2015.

## Tony Faust: A Taste of Heaven

"Elizabeth Terry Speaks on Faust Family, May 4, 2015." Sappington-Concord Historical Society, http://www.schs.ws/schs2/elizabeth-terry-speaks-on-faust-family/. Accessed January 22, 2016.

"Faust Park." St. Louis County, Missouri, Parks and Recreation, http://www.stlouisco.com/parksandrecreation/parkpages/faust. Accessed January 22, 2016.

Merkel, Jim. *Beer, Brats, and Baseball: German-Americans in St. Louis,* 2nd ed. St. Louis: Reedy Press, 2015.

"Reintroducing Faust to St. Louis." Anheuser-Busch Newsroom, March 13, 2015. Accessed January 22, 2016.

*St. Louis Post-Dispatch.* November 11, 1949.

Terry, Elizabeth. *Oysters to Angus: Three Generations of the St. Louis Faust Family.* St. Louis: Bluebird Publishing, 2014.

## Tom Goabout: Champion of the Poultry Pilferers

*St. Louis Post-Dispatch.* May 30, 1885; December 9, 1888; November 20, 1892; May 13, 1894; December 11, 1897; December 13, 1897; August 20, 1898; April 3, 1900; June 16, 1900; November 29, 1900; June 16, 1903; June 25, 2012.

## Will Greensburg: A Newsie Makes It Big

"Rolla Wells." St. Louis Public Library, http://exhibits.slpl.org/mayors. Accessed October 16, 2015.

*St. Louis Post-Dispatch.* February 25, 1909; June 15, 1911; September 25, 1911; December 27, 1911; June 12, 1917.

*St. Louis Republic.* September 25, 1911; unknown date, September 1911.

U.S. Inflation Calculator. http://www.usinflationcalculator.com/. Accessed October 16, 2015.

## Robert "Hot Rod" Moore: Flooring It on Portland Place

"Missouri Department of Revenue Tickets and Points FAQs." http://dor.mo.gov/faq/drivers/points.php. Accessed September 20, 2015, and June 10, 2016.

*St. Louis Globe-Democrat.* May 14, 1951; July 16, 1951; August 1, 1953; April 16, 1954; September 16, 1954; October 28, 1954.

*St. Louis Post-Dispatch.* August 31, 1950; March 14, 1951; September 1, 1954; January 11, 1998.

## Owen Dacey: Dancing through His Duty

"Pop Cop—A Film by Don Pietromonaco 1968." https://www.youtube.com/watch?v=WeifPwtsVTQ. Accessed March 2, 2016.

*Prescott [Arizona] Courier.* September 30, 1971.

*St. Louis Post-Dispatch.* May 14, 1967; May 21, 2014; May 22, 2014.

"The Dancing Policeman, St. Louis Metropolitan Police Department." https://www.youtube.com/watch?v=3bSKC6xueZg. Accessed March 2, 2016.

## Tony Gagliarducci: Keeping Sharp on the South Side

Business card of Tony Gagliarducci, knife sharpener. Missouri History Museum Archives.

Gregali, Stephen M. Correspondence. September 19, 2015.

Lubbock [Texas] Avalanche-Journal. July 13, 2009.

Photograph and catalog record of grinder cart operated by Anthony Gagliarducci. Missouri History Museum website. http://collections.mohistory.org/resource/197945.html. Accessed August 10, 2016.

South Side Journal. November 16, 1985.

St. Louis Post-Dispatch. March 4, 1991.

## Charles Hoessle: Snake Man

Hoessle, Charles. Interview with follow-up interviews. November 9, 2015.

## Bucket Joe: The Most Famous Homeless Man in St. Louis

Merkel, Jim. Hoosiers and Scrubby Dutch: St. Louis's South Side, 2nd ed. St. Louis: Reedy Press, 2014.

## Bob Cassilly: An Ageless Kid on a Playground

Cassilly, Max. Interview. Circa January 26, 2016.

Christman, Bill. Interviews with follow-ups. May 25 and May 31, 2016.

City Museum. http://www.citymuseum.org/. Accessed June 6, 2016.

Erwin, Rick. Interview. Circa January 27, 2016.

Fontbonne University. "History of Fontbonne University." https://www.fontbonne.edu/about/history-of-fontbonne-university/. Accessed June 13, 2016.

Fowler, Nancy. "Cassilly Remembered as Visionary, Force of Nature." St. Louis Beacon, https://www.stlbeacon.org/#!/content/15160/cassilly_remembered_as_visionary_force_of_nature. Accessed January 30–31, 2016.

Riverfront Times. October 6, 2011.

Singer, Dale. "Bob Cassilly, Founder of City Museum, Found Dead in Bulldozer at His Cementland Project." St. Louis Beacon, https://www.stlbeacon.org/#!/content/15162/bob_cassilly_founder_of_city_museum_dies_in_accident_at_former_cement_plant. Accessed January 31, 2016.

*St. Louis Post-Dispatch*. July 28, 1993; April 25, 1994; August 28, 1994; September 22, 1994; April 13, 2007; October 18, 2007; September 27, 2011.

*West County Journal*. April 13, 1994.

## Tom Dunn: River Man

Dunn, Tom. Interviews and correspondence. May–June 2016.

Dunn, J. Thomas. *Admiral: A Book Full of Memories*. Florissant, Missouri: Little River Books, 2014.

## Joe Edwards: How to Be *Loopish*

Edwards, Joe. Interviews. August 14, 2015; June 9, 2016.

Bryant, Tim. "In Just 15 Months, Rock & Roll Beer Has . . ." www.upi.com/ Archives/1983/06/09/In-just-15-months-Rock-Roll-beer-has/ 9805423979200/. Accessed June 11, 2016.

Moonrise Hotel brochure. visittheloop.com. Accessed August 16, 2015.

## George Simon: Patriarch of the Mangoes and Pears

Inserra-Meyer, Rosina. Interview. November 2015.

Simon, George. Interview. November 2015.

Spinks, Darryl. Interview. November 2015.

Wheelock, Roy. Interview. November 2015.

Winebright, Brenda. Interview with follow-up conversation and correspondence. November 2015.

## Albert Watkins: Toe Smasher at Law

Cooperman, Jeannette. "A Conversation with Albert Watkins." *St. Louis Magazine*, March 26, 2010. http://www.stlmag.com/Q-ampA-Albert-Watkins/. Accessed February 25, 2016.

Fact sheet of major cases of Albert S. Watkins, given to the author by Watkins during February 22, 2016, interview.

Harris, Joe. "South Butt Clothing Falls off a Cliff." Courthouse News Service, October 17, 2012, http://www.courthousenews. com/2012/10/17/51356.htm. Accessed February 25. 2016.

Kodner Watkins LC. http://kwklaw.net/attorneys/bios/albert-watkins. Accessed February 25, 2016.

Letter from Albert S. Watkins to Martin D. Singer, Issued in Furtherance of Settlement Undertakings Not Evidentiary in Nature, October 14, 2013.

Letter from Albert S. Watkins to Mayor Shelly Welsch, February 24, 2016. https://www.scribd.com/doc/300318937/Open-Letter-to-Mayor-of-U-City. Accessed August 10, 2016.

Phillips, Nicholas. "A Heated Deposition Turns the South Butt Case Into One Giant 'Clusterf@#k.'" *Riverfront Times*, March 23, 2010. http://www.riverfronttimes.com/newsblog/2010/03/23/a-heated-deposition-turns-the-south-butt-case-into-one-giant-clusterfk?page=2. Accessed February 25, 2016.

"Quote of the Day: South Butt vs. North Face Is A 'Monumental Clusterf#@k.'" http://mobile.businessinsider.com/quote-of-the-day-south-butt-v-north-face-is-a-monumental-clusterfk-2010-3. Accessed February 25, 2016.

*St. Louis Post-Dispatch*. January 6, 2010; December 21, 2011; February 11, 2014; February 23, 2016.

"The Strughold Story." Copyrighted manuscript detailing the case of James E. Strughold, given to the author during February 22, 2016, interview.

Watkins, Albert. Interview with follow-up correspondence and interviews. February 22, 2016.

## Raynard Nebbitt: That Guy on the Overpass

Nebbitt, Raynard, and Kathy Nebbitt. Interview with follow-up questions. October 6, 2015.

*Webster-Kirkwood Times*. June 24, 2005.

## Bill Christman: An Artiste and a Jokester

Christman, Bill. Interviews with follow-ups. May 25 and May 31, 2016.

Christman, Mary. Interview. May 31, 2016.

Merkel, Jim. "Cherokee Street Sculptor Is His Own Worst Critic." *Suburban Journals of Greater St. Louis*, June 1, 2007. http://www.stltoday.com/suburban-journals/cherokee-street-sculptor-is-his-own-worst-critic/article_c1a4b734-e38e-506b-a85e-5e2bede43963.html. Accessed June 5, 2016.

## Paul "Father Time" Pagano: Everyone's Goodwill Ambassador

Pagano, John. Interview. January 17, 2016.

Pagano, Paul. Interview. January 8, 2016.

*St. Louis Post-Dispatch*. January 1, 2006.

## Steven Fitzpatrick Smith: Weatherman

"Democratic Caucus Returns at the Royale and Iowa Caucus Returns Watch." https://www.facebook.com/events/921015387975071/. Accessed February 27, 2016.

Merkel, Jim. *Hoosiers and Scrubby Dutch: St. Louis's South Side*, 2nd ed. St. Louis: Reedy Press, 2014.

Roberts, Randall. "The Boxers' Rebellion." *Riverfront Times*, April 2, 2003. http://m.riverfronttimes.com/stlouis/the-boxers-rebellion/Content?oid=2466289. Accessed February 28, 2016.

Smith, Steven Fitzpatrick. Interview with follow-up interviews. February 23, 2016.

"Steven Fitzpatrick Smith Floorlength Urinal Posts." Facebook page. https://www.facebook.com/search/top/?q=%20steven%20fitzpatrick%20smith%20floorlength%20urinal. Accessed February 29, 2016.

"The Royale." Facebook page, January 31, 2016. https://www.facebook.com/royalestl/posts/10153790370492209. Accessed February 26, 2016.

# PHOTO CREDITS

Any photos not listed below are believed to be in the public domain.

# INDEX